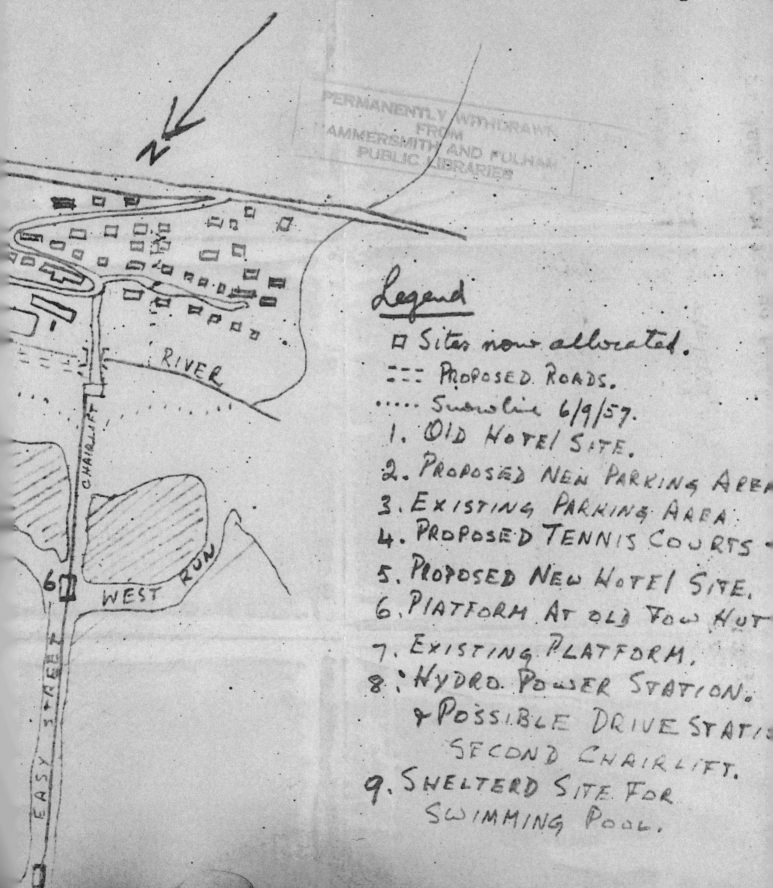

PERMANENTLY WITHDRAWN
FROM
HAMMERSMITH AND FULHAM
PUBLIC LIBRARIES

D1685662

N

RIVER

CHAIRLIFT

WEST RUN

6

EASY STREET

Legend

☐ Sites now allocated.

≡≡≡ PROPOSED ROADS.

····· Snowline 6/9/57.

1. OLD HOTEL SITE.

2. PROPOSED NEW PARKING AREA

3. EXISTING PARKING AREA.

4. PROPOSED TENNIS COURTS.

5. PROPOSED NEW HOTEL SITE.

6. PLATFORM AT OLD TOW HUT

7. EXISTING PLATFORM.

8. HYDRO. POWER STATION.
  & POSSIBLE DRIVE STATION
  SECOND CHAIRLIFT.

9. SHELTERD SITE FOR
  SWIMMING POOL.

Thredbo **50**

tSm Publishing Pty Ltd
12 Alton Road (PO Box 146),
Mt Macedon, 3441, Victoria, Australia
Tel: (03) 5426 2578
www.theskimag.com

Published by tSm Publishing Pty Ltd, 2006

Copyright © 2006, Jim Darby and Kosciuszko Thredbo Pty Ltd

Kosciuszko Thredbo Pty Ltd
Valley Terminal
(PO Box 92)
Thredbo, 2625, NSW, Australia
Tel: (02) 6459 4100
www.thredbo.com.au

National Library of Australia Cataloguing-in-Publication
Data:
Darby, Jim, 1957-

Thredbo 50.
Bibliography.
Includes index.

ISBN 0 646 46813 8

1. Thredbo Alpine Resort (NSW) - History. 2. Ski resorts -
New South Wales - Thredbo - History. 3. Mountain resorts -
New South Wales - Thredbo - History. 4. Thredbo (NSW) -
History. I. Title.

919.447062

All rights reserved. Without limiting the rights under
copyright reserved above, no part of this publication may
be reproduced, stored in or introduced into a retrieval
system, or transmitted in any form or by any means
(electronically, photocopying, mechanically, recording or
otherwise) without the prior written permission of both the
above copyright owners.

Designed, produced and printed in Australia.

Typeset in Avenir LT Book, 9/14

Publisher's note: This is a historic work. Every effort has been
made to ensure the accuracy of the information contained
herein and acknowledge its source, however the publisher
cannot accept responsibility for any errors or omissions.
Every effort has been made to trace copyright owners in
pictorial works; sources for pictorial works are acknowledged
on page 121.

Thredbo **50**

1957 to 2007

Jim Darby

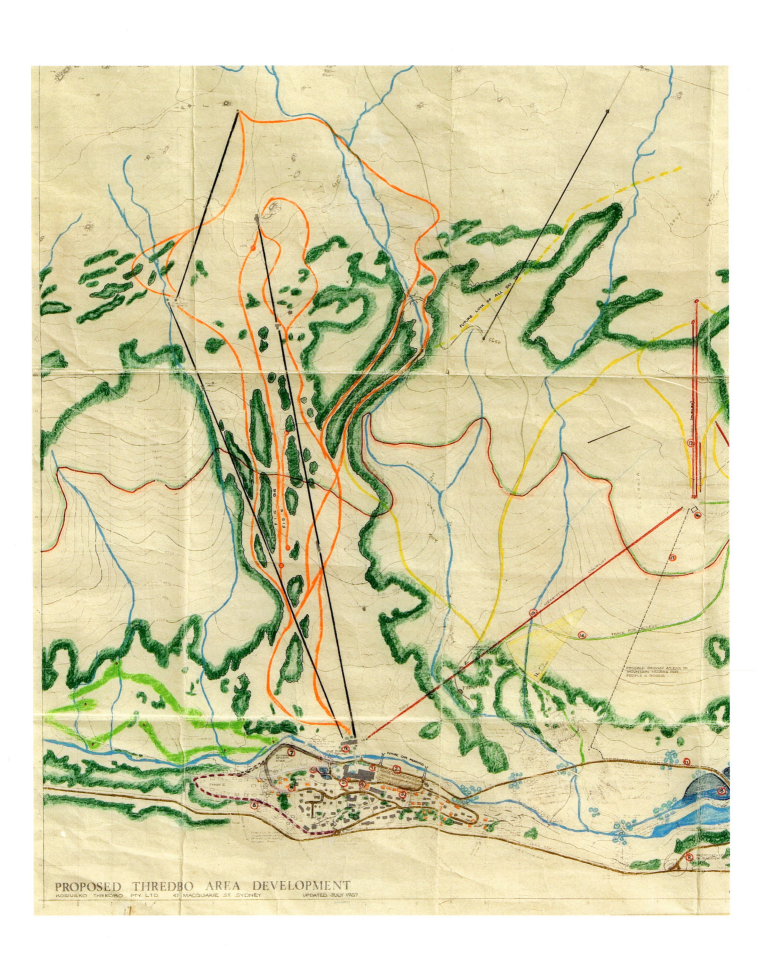

PROPOSED THREDBO AREA DEVELOPMENT

KOSIUSKO THREDBO PTY. LTD.   47 MACQUARIE ST. SYDNEY   UPDATED JULY 1967

Contents

COVERS: *The Crackenback rope tow (front cover) was Thredbo's first lift, open for business in the 1957 winter. The resort was thriving in the 1960s (back cover), with a growing village and chairlifts including Ramshead and Crackenback.*

NATURAL HORIZONS: *On page 3 is a summer rainbow over Thredbo; on page 5 are the granite tors of the Ramshead Range; and on the previous spread is a young Thredbo River.*

MAKING PLANS: *At left is the distillation of the Lend Lease Thredbo master plan, developed in the early 1960s and illustrated in this way in 1967. The sketch plan on the inside front cover is from the records of John Gam, a skifields engineer and original shareholder in Kosciuszko Thredbo, it was probably drawn late in 1959. On the inside back cover is Thredbo's 2006 trail map.*

Discovery

Australia in the 1950s was a mix of austerity and adventure, recovery and growth, careful progress and bold ambitions. People were thriving on the promise of peace after a brutal world war but were thrifty in the face of scarce resources. In the Snowy Mountains, skiing was still the domain of a small band of enthusiasts, constrained not so much by cost or class-based exclusivity as the availability of facilities as basic as shelter.

Despite the constraints, skiers were pushing the boundaries, moving beyond the traditional base at the Kosciuszko Chalet at Charlotte Pass to build outposts of mountain huts such as Kunama and Albina; taking advantage of the more reliable snow cover and more challenging slopes in these alpine areas closer to Australia's summit – Mt Kosciuszko.

They used these huts as bases to explore even further into the mountains, to find longer and even more challenging runs. They shared the thirst for variety and adventure that still grips skiers and snowboarders.

Geoffrey Hughes, a founding director of Thredbo and a member of the Ski Tourers' Association (STA), recalled skiing the slopes on the Ramshead Range high above the Thredbo River in the early 1950s.

One destination on the Ramshead Range was Twin Valleys, down river from Thredbo and Merritts Spur – they called it the George Chisholm course and ran the Australian championships there in 1953 and 1954.

It was named after an influential skier and early Australian Winter Olympic team manager.

To get there from the STA's Kunama Hutte, Hughes recalled skiing 'down from Kunama to the Snowy River and there was a suspension bridge over the Snowy.'

They would then climb up to the ridge, have a practice run, pack the course 'and then you'd have your run and that'd be it. It was pretty hairy, it was quite a good downhill course,' Hughes said.

For competitive skiing, there was a sheltered downhill course close to the chalet at Charlotte Pass, but there were no big slopes, no dramatic, long and steep runs. On the Ramshead Range 'you were getting big slopes with a lot of vertical drop,' Hughes said.

The course-setter for the 1954 Australian Downhill Championships on the George Chisholm course was a former Czech Olympic skier, Tony Sponar. He described the course as a '… setter's dream with changes of gradients, gullies and belts of trees.' (Sponar p123).

With his British wife Lizi (Elizabeth), Tony Sponar had migrated to Australia in 1950 and in 1951 found work in the Snowy Mountains, at the Hotel Kosciuszko on the Kosciuszko Road, where Sponars Chalet operates today. Only a few months after their arrival, the hotel was

THE VISION: *Tony Sponar (at left) and Charles Anton consider the options as they look up at the Ramshead Range in 1955. The muddy track they are standing on was bulldozed off the Alpine Way; crucial access for their own adventures and to open up the Thredbo Valley.*

Ski THREDBO this year!

AUSTRALIA'S NEWEST AND GREATEST ALPINE RESORT

New mile long double chair-lift, rising 1,540 feet. Also rope tow and T-Bar lift.

★

Slopes of every gradient— up to 2,500 feet descent.

★

Accommodation for 200 people at Thredbo Village.

★

Ski school—chief instructor, Leonhard Erhater, of Zurs, Austria.

★

22 miles from Jinda-byne on the Alpine Way, an all weather road; 157 miles from Albury via Geehi.

General Booking Agents :

World Travel Head-quarters, A.P.A. Building, Martin Place, Sydney, BW 4841; 346 Little Collins St., Melbourne, MU 7188. You can book also at all leading Travel Agents and Ski shops.

IMPORTANT: The second subdivision of building sites at Thredbo Village will be made shortly. Ski clubs and other interested persons are invited to apply for details to the Secretary, Kosciusko Thredbo Ltd., 65 York Street, Sydney, N.S.W.

!09

THE MESSAGE: *Thredbo advertising in the Australian Ski Yearbook, introducing the resort in 1958 (left) and detailing its progress and achievements in 1963 (bottom right).*

destroyed by fire and the Sponars were transferred to the Kosciuszko Chalet at Charlotte Pass where they spent the winter of 1951.

This gave Tony Sponar his introduction to Australia's skiing fraternity and also a sense of the potential of the sport and its industry.

His background in competitive skiing and as a ski instructor at St Anton in Austria's Arlberg gave him a depth of understanding few would have shared at the time.

Sponar wrote that, in their 'first weekend at the chalet, a short, noisy man appeared. In no time, he had introduced himself as Charles Anton and just as fast, he had told me that I should be the one to help him with his current project.' (Sponar, p21).

The project he referred to was the construction of the Lake Albina Ski Lodge, on the flank of Mt Northcote near Mt Townsend.

Anton was born in Austria in 1916, the son of a Jewish timber-merchant. He left Austria in the late 1930s follow-

ing the Anschluss or Nazi annexation and eventually enlisted in the Australian Military Forces, skiing for the army team in 1945.

He had a gift for organising people and it was that gift that underpinned the success of the STA, which he later transformed into the Australian Alpine Club.

Sponar wrote, 'Charles and I would become closer in the near future. He would talk about his plans and I would talk about my dream. I was looking for a place where the ski runs would be long and challenging, easily accessible, and where you could establish a modern winter resort.' (Sponar, p24).

During that first winter at the chalet, Sponar recalled a skier whose 'name I have long forgotten … pointed his hand towards the south and said, "There, past those ranges is a deep valley. There are very long slopes before you reach the river on the bottom",' (Sponar, p34).

He realised this was the Ramshead Range and the Thredbo River valley. In the summer of 1951-52 Sponar wrote that he frequented the area, spending almost as much effort navigating his way in and out as inspecting the terrain and judging its potential.

Parallel with this deepening penetration of skiers into the Snowy Mountains was a much more dramatic incursion – that amazing engineering feat of the era, the Snowy Mountains Hydro-Electric Scheme.

As well as building the crucial infrastructure – such as the Alpine Way up the Thredbo Valley and over the mountains towards Victoria – the scheme drew many of the people who would eventually shape the mountain resorts. It employed more than 100,000 workers from 30 different countries.

Sponar moved from the chalet to work with the Snowy Mountains Scheme, eventually as a hydrographer, enabling him to travel throughout the mountains as he measured stream flows. He recalled passing the

Kosciuszko Chalet during the 1954 winter when a fellow former Czech Olympian, Sasha Nekvapil, who was working there as a ski instructor, introduced him to a Sydney-based architect, Eric Nicholls who was holidaying at the chalet with his wife.

Sponar described his dream to Nicholls – a place with a site for a European-style mountain village in its valley floor and a mountain range with the vertical drop and variety in its terrain for good skiing.

Access was crucial in the transformation of Sponar's vision. In his 1954 conversation with Nicholls, he recalled telling him that the 'Snowy Mountains Authority would begin construction of a road through the valley shortly.' (Sponar, p129).

Nicholls was inspired by Sponar's proposal and committed to generating some publicity for it and also agreed to try and locate chairlift manufacturers they might be able to engage.

Nicholls had been in partnership with Walter Burley Griffin and, having worked on projects such as Sydney's Castlecrag development in the 1930s, understood what was involved in generating support for a major development and in steering the difficult course through the approval process.

In April 1955, Nicholls met in Sydney with Geoffrey Hughes and Charles Anton who knew each other through the STA. Hughes, a Sydney solicitor, recalled saying during that meeting 'if you want to do something, we've got to form a syndicate and get ourselves a business name and go to the Park Trust and say to them, "OK, we want to do something in the Thredbo (Valley), what's the deal?"'

So in May 1955, Charles Anton, Geoffrey Hughes, Eric Nicholls and Tony Sponar formed the Kosciuszko Chairlift and Thredbo Hotel syndicate. Nicholls insisted on the inclusion of Kosciuszko in the syndicate name, anticipating the publicity in the association with Australia's highest mountain.

They approached the Kosciuszko State Park Trust. The Trust had an obligation to promote tourism in the area, so were not opposed to the syndicate's plans, but they were sceptical about their ability to implement them.

'The Park Trust said "well, what are you going to do for money?"' Geoffrey Hughes said. 'We said, "well, we'll issue a prospectus and the skiers will give us the money." The park chaps said, "ha, ha – go and find someone with some real money to back you".'

Hughes started to approach some of the people he knew or knew of in Sydney to see if he could stimulate their interest. 'One was Walter McGrath who was chairman of Lennons Hotel, he said "no, the snow's no good, it's too seasonal, you want to invest in the seaside, we're going to build a big hotel at a place called Surfer's Paradise."

'The other one I went to was Alan Murray-Jones who was the boss of de Havillands at Bankstown. Like my father, he had been a pilot in France in the First World War and he said he'd think about who could help.

'He came back to me a little later and said "Thyne Reid might be your man".'

Andrew Thyne Reid was chairman of the company then known as James Hardie Asbestos, and Hughes discovered he was also a member of the Ski Club of Australia (SCA), so he contacted Bertie (Sir Herbert) Schlink, the president of the SCA and, through him, arranged a dinner with Thyne Reid.

Thredbo

ALPINE VILLAGE

NEW!
NEW SKI LIFTS!
NEW "A" CLASS HOTEL!
NEW BEGINNER SLOPES!
NEW EASIER ACCESS!
NEW EASIER PARKING!

This year Thredbo Alpine Village will be better than ever. New ski lifts are being installed . . . exciting new slopes opened up. A new Hotel and enlarged Guest Lodges offer economy to luxurious accommodation to suit your pocket . . . and a new all-weather access road and ample provision for parking enables you to leave your car just a few yards from your accommodation and the ski lifts.

And at night you will enjoy the gaiety, glamour and carefree relaxation of the after-ski hours . . . an evening spent by a roaring lodge fire . . . a drink with a new friend . . . an impromptu party or a dance.

You may come to Thredbo as a stranger but you will leave it as a friend. For skiers are that sort of people and Thredbo is that kind of place.

THREDBO BOOKING CENTRE

Sydney: Kindersley House, 33 Bligh Street, Sydney. 'Phone: BW 5809

Melbourne: Deans Building, Little Collins Street, Melbourne. 'Phone: MU 7188

or your Local Travel Agent

NEW HOTEL. The new Thredbo Coach House Inn provides international standards of snow-resort luxury. Each room has its own private bathroom.

NEW SKI LIFTS. The new chair lift and T-bar will double Thredbo's up-hill capacity. The lifts are capable of carrying over 2,000 skiers per hour and provide the best lift facilities anywhere in the Southern Alps.

SKI HIRE. The best ski-equipment — imported skis with safety bindings, double padded boots and stocks for hire at 90/- a week. Waterproof parkas and ski-pants also for hire. Bookings from Thredbo Booking Centre or phone BW 1111.

SKI LODGES. Thredbo's attractive guest lodges — Sasha's, Christiana, Candlelight, Leo's, Lentern, Alpenhorn and The Silver Brumby — offer a wide selection of accommodation.

SKI SCHOOL. Thredbo's famous ski school under the direction of world-famous Austrian ski expert Leon Erharter will soon have you skiing expertly. Special classes for all grades. Private lessons may be booked in advance.

Exciting new beginners' slopes are being opened and whether you are a beginner or Olympic champion, you will find the lift and terrain to best suit your ability.

13

Thyne Reid had access to the finance and was in a position to guarantee the syndicate's bank account. 'Without him, we wouldn't have got it off the ground,' Hughes said.

In May 1955, the syndicate formally applied to the Park Trust for a lease – it took another two and a half years for the lease to come through, but the Park Trust gave the syndicate permission to start implementing its proposal for a hotel and chairlift. While they were agreed on the broad area, they had to pinpoint the site for their village. 'We'd originally talked about the George Chisholm course,' Geoffrey Hughes said, 'but we decided there was not enough flat land to have summer activities – tennis courts, golf course.

'You had to have summer activities otherwise you're dead in the water … at Thredbo year round usage was always part of the plan. We found a certain amount of flat land … with good slopes and the possibility of getting up into the very high stuff.'

Anton and Hughes made frequent trips with Sponar during the winter of 1955, but it was not until September 1955 that they saw the Friday Flat area, the site of an SMA camp, as the best prospect for their alpine village.

In an article in the 1956 *Australian Ski Year Book*, Hughes wrote that this was '… quite the most pleasant part of the Thredbo Valley, for while most of the valley is wild and rugged, Friday Flat is peaceful and park-like.'

'After another survey trip and much discussion, we chose as the site of the proposed chairlift a ridge about three miles (5km) below Dead Horse Gap. At the top of this ridge is a peak 6400 feet (1952m) high which we have named Crackenback Peak.'

The jigsaw was coming together – with 'Crackenback Peak' agreed to as the summit of the chairlift and Friday Flat the preferred site for a village, it was simply a matter of connecting the two.

(The peak referred to in the early days as Crackenback Peak is the unnamed peak above Thredbo's Eagles Nest – the actual Crackenback Peak, as gazetted by the NSW Department of Lands is much farther down river, above Penderlea and Crackenback Farm. Along the same lines, the area then known as Friday Flat encompassed the whole of what is now Thredbo Village, rather than the smaller area that is now known as Friday Flat.)

VALLEY VIEW: *The Thredbo Valley and the Ramshead Range, looking from the NSW end of the valley into Victoria. The earliest skiers would trek over from the Kosciuszko Chalet or Kunama Hutte, in the mountains to the right of this photo.*
Competitive skiing was held on the George Chisholm course, down river from Thredbo where the valley tightens. The flatter land around the Friday Flat camp, where the rows of cars sit in this picture, was a key factor in the syndicate selecting this site.

The syndicate members debated the exact location of the hotel – whether it would be on the north bank (lift side) or south bank. Either with an eye for compromise or for architectural splendour, Sponar recalled Thyne Reid suggesting the hotel should 'straddle the Thredbo River.' (Sponar p143). Perhaps with the obstacle of the river and the cost of bridging it in mind and perhaps because it was the sunnier side, the area south of the river was chosen for the hotel and village.

In the summer of 1955-56, for a cost of £218, including a £5 worker's compensation policy, a survey line was cleared by Tony Sponar, Jindabyne-based skier Danny

Collman and some SMA workers for what was intended to be the Crackenback chairlift.

This line was about 150m upriver from the eventual lift line and although it was truer to the fall line than the route eventually followed, there was little flat land at its base.

It was abandoned and another line cut early in the summer of 1956-57, which was used for the rope tow – it is the line still followed by the Kosciuszko Express chairlift.

On May 17, 1957, the syndicate was incorporated as Kosciuszko Thredbo Limited. Its shareholders were Eric Nicholls, Geoffrey Hughes, Andrew Thyne Reid, Charles Anton, John Gam, an engineer who was starting to spe-

cialise in ski lift construction, George Lloyd, a Sydney businessman, and Dawn Hughes, Geoffrey Hughes' wife. Tony Sponar was appointed area manager.

In November 1957, the company was granted a lease by the NSW Minister for Lands which gave it various rights over ski lifts, ski tows, liquor sales, a service station and the rights to sub-divide, develop or sub-lease 67 acres (28 hectares) of land in the valley for the village and rights over 4570 acres (1850 hectares) surrounding it for the skifield.

That land was available to the company for five years. In that time, Kosciuszko Thredbo had to build a chairlift one mile long and a hotel of at least 80 beds. If it achieved these milestones, it was then in a position to secure a 99-year lease.

Financing the development remained a major challenge, so in March 1958, the company issued a prospectus, offering 100,000 ordinary £1 shares. It proudly announced its program to develop Australia's largest chairlift, rising 1540' (470m) some smaller ski lifts, a licensed hotel, an alpine village with shops and all services, leasing of lodge sites to ski clubs and other interested persons, operation of a ski school and 'further development of trout fishing and other summer attractions.'

'It didn't raise much dough,' Geoffrey Hughes said. 'It was fairly understandable – after the Kunama disaster (see chapter two), skiing didn't exactly seem to be a gold-plated investment opportunity.'

While the village grew, with more and more sites allocat-

ed to clubs and the chairlift replacing the rope tow, the company couldn't generate the money it needed to fulfill its development obligations.

Friction between the directors and their area manager saw Sponar moved aside in 1958. He and Lizi ran one of the new commercial lodges – Bursills – for a time but they eventually left Thredbo to resurrect what had been the Kosciuszko Hotel and transform it into Sponars Chalet on the Kosciuszko Road.

For his role in Thredbo's establishment, Sponar had been granted 4000 shares in Kosciuszko Thredbo. Thyne Reid bought the shares for £4000 in what was regarded as an act of considerable generosity and fair play.

As a point of comparison, following a skiing accident around this time, Geoffrey Hughes sold some of his shares to help him through his rehabilitation and received 10 shillings (half the amount paid to Sponar) for each share.

The vision Sponar shared with his fellow pioneers would be realised, but he would play little further part in its realisation.

The company had the chairlift built, but by 1960, the deadline to also have the hotel in place was looming and it became apparent to Kosciuszko Thredbo's directors that they simply lacked the resources.

Their chairman, Thyne Reid, decided to see if he could get a takeover bid and he uncovered two – Lend Lease and Coach House Motor Inns.

Lend Lease was the highest bidder. It bought out the founding shareholder group and set about making its own plans for Thredbo. Lend Lease had been formed in 1958. The engineering and construction company, Civil & Civic was the major shareholder in Lend Lease.

Civil & Civic itself was formed in 1951 – its first contract was to supply and build 200 prefabricated houses for the Snowy Mountains Authority and it won the contract in

IN LINE: *Constance Hughes Crisp walks the line of the Crackenback rope tow, Easter 1957, a line the Kosciuszko Express still follows. At its base is an almost completed Crackenback Ski Club lodge and the foundations of the syndicate's Thredbo Lodge.*

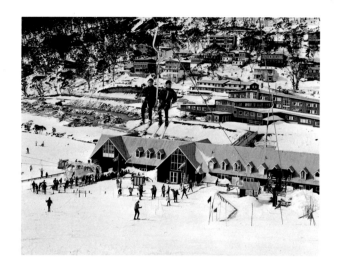

NEW LEASE: *A period of intense development followed the Lend Lease takeover in 1961, with the original chairlift extended, Ramshead chairlift and Valley Terminal (in the foreground here) built and the first stage of the hotel completed. This photograph was probably taken in 1964.*

1959 for stage one of the Sydney Opera House.

In 1961, in what we now might call a reverse takeover, Lend Lease bought Civil & Civic from the Dutch building company, Bredero's.

In the early 1950s, Bredero's had sent Gerardus Dusseldorp – Duss or Dick was how he became known in Australia – to assess the market opportunities in Australia and work as construction manager for Civil & Civic.

Dusseldorp went on to run Lend Lease and exploited those market opportunities in brilliant form, completing major construction projects such as Sydney's Caltex House in 1957 with architect Eric Nichols and Australia Square in 1968.

In 1961, Lend Lease took over Kosciuszko Thredbo and immediately applied its depth in engineering, construction and project planning, along with its financial resources, which were significantly greater than those available to the resort's founders.

He wasn't a skier, so Dusseldorp assessed Thredbo purely from a business perspective; his judgement was not coloured by any passion for snowsports.

'I thought the lease with the government was a very favourable lease. It was designed by people that didn't know what they were doing, but I could see there were benefits if you did it in a properly financed way,' Dusseldorp said in a 1995 interview.

Towards the end of winter 1962, one of Civil & Civic's Sydney Opera House engineers, Albert van der Lee, moved to Thredbo to first work as site engineer, then resident engineer and eventually general manager for Kosciuszko Thredbo.

'Quite a crew went from the Sydney Opera House to Thredbo,' van der Lee said. Their immediate tasks were to build the second stage of the Thredbo Alpine Hotel and extend the chairlift beyond Kareela station.

By doing this, Dusseldorp was in a position to negotiate the head lease for Thredbo with the NSW Government – a 45-year lease with an option for a further 50 years. It is this head lease agreement that sets Thredbo apart from virtually all other Australian mountain resorts. It was partly inherited from the resort's founders and their agreements with the Park Trust and partly adapted from Lend Lease's property ventures.

'The company would construct shopping centres and sign a head lease with the owner of the shopping centre – an institution for instance – and then lease the centre from the owner to manage it at a profit. Lend Lease would then sub-lease the shops and spaces to various smaller businesses. That was really an invention of Lend Lease in the early 1960s,' Albert van der Lee said.

The Park Trust had an obligation to improve public facilities in the park but it lacked the resources. What they were able to give was the only thing they had to offer – longevity of tenure and certainty over rental and development rights.

David Osborn, Kosciuszko Thredbo's managing director in the 1990s, said that even then, the head lease gave them the luxury of longevity.

'Duss had created the base so whenever we thought strategically, we could think about how something would contribute to Thredbo in 20 and 30 years time, not just in the next four years.'

DISCOVERY

The advantage for the Parks Trust was that it only had to deal with one company and it wasn't responsible for infrastructure. At other NSW resorts, the National Parks and Wildlife Service has spent millions taking care of municipal services such as rubbish, water and sewerage. At Thredbo it has no responsibility in these areas.

The Thredbo model is the envy of all other major Australian alpine resort operators and it isn't just about revenue – although that is significant because, as Osborn said, 'control of revenue means you can take the big decisions and get the money back from the big investments.'

In the running of the resort however, where service is paramount to the success of the business, the crucial difference is that Thredbo can control the guests' experience. Kosciuszko Thredbo runs the lifts but it also leases out the restaurants, parks the cars, and employs the ski

patrol, ski instructors and lift operators – it retains the dominant influence over the customer's day 'and that means you can control the quality of the service.'

'In Thredbo,' Osborn said, 'we could make a decision to spend $6 or $7 million on an alpine training centre – it added value to our land, was part of our summer business and indirectly through all the lodges and the retail, some of the money was coming back to us. If the lift company in another resort did that, what would they get back? The $2 entry fee?

'The difference is critical to understanding why Thredbo is the way it is.'

With the lease secured, Dusseldorp sought to establish a master plan for Thredbo. He travelled down from Sydney every weekend for two years, usually with his family, and he and Albert van der Lee would clamber over the moun-

tain until they knew every rock on it – 'we had to walk and climb it all before making these commitments. It was a very big financial commitment – the commercial necessity was that you had to do it yourself,' Dusseldorp said.

For the skifields development, they consulted heavily with Austrian ski instructor and Thredbo ski school director, Leonard Erharter. 'We recognised his experience and leaned heavily on his knowledge,' Dusseldorp said.

All this exploration and expertise was distilled into Thredbo's 1967 Master Plan and while subsequent plans have added to it and re-shaped it, the 1967 plan remains the fundamental blueprint for Thredbo.

In 1995, on a return visit to Thredbo, Dusseldorp was shown the resort's latest Master Plan and he said 'hey, that's our plan from 1967.' And when they compared the plans, they found that was indeed the foundation for the new one.

Dusseldorp was a powerful leader for Thredbo. He would speak about hardware and software; physical structures such as lifts and buildings on the one hand and ideas and applications on the other; about how an asset could be extended.

Like its founders, he always recognised Thredbo's year-round potential. 'That was one of the major reasons of buying-in,' Dusseldorp said.

THE RIVER RUNS THROUGH IT: *Entirely surrounded by the Kosciuszko National Park, Thredbo's natural environment, the river, the valley and the mountain range that dominates it has always been at the heart of its appeal.*

'We knew we'd be buying in to a lot of trouble – in fact we never made a profit for 10 years – but the summer potential I considered to exceed that of the winter. Winter is limited in the Australian Alps, summer is unique.'

Backing that principle, very early in the piece he decided the chairlift should run from daylight to dusk – all day, every day.

'There were days when not a soul would go on that, but we ran it. Tour operators and bus tour people learned to believe that they could sell that in their little tour – a trip on the chairlift at Thredbo,' Albert van der Lee said.

He was a tough negotiator, but Dusseldorp also had a fierce regard for fair dealing.

In a company town, which with its head lease, Thredbo essentially is, the head of the company effectively becomes the community's mayor.

'Some people called me that,' van der Lee said, 'but it was not a big problem, it didn't stop me from making friends there and most of the situations could be sorted out with common sense. Of course, I had the advantage that I had to follow the rules that were established from above and behave ethically.

'That was hammered into us by Dusseldorp – you had to have community spirit and if you were ethical, it was virtually impossible to get into trouble,' van der Lee said.

While he saw summer as broadening the base, Dusseldorp anticipated the market growth in skiing – 'that was very easy to see,' he said, 'the constant growth in popularity was only restrained in Australia because there were no snowfields. The Snowy Mountains (scheme) opened that up and then the nation had to learn what it was like.'

For Albert van der Lee, the immediate tasks were to get the infrastructure in place, to replace septic tanks with an effective sewerage system for the village, to create an effective water supply system and secure the electricity supply (moving with the times, Nicholls and Anton had planned on a hydro-electric scheme, but this was never implemented).

When his role changed to become Kosciuszko Thredbo's resident engineer, van der Lee had to sort out the subdivision of the village land and attempt to fill the vacant blocks.

Before Lend Lease took over, it had not quite been a free-for-all, but with few resources to manage the development

OPTIONS: *In the 1958 winter, skiers Jane Tinsley (left) and Pat Barker contemplate the possibilities – this photo first appeared in* The Sydney Morning Herald. *In 2006, snowboarder Amy Smith and skier Stacey Nicholson do the same – behind them is a walking map for summer visitors.*

of the village, the boundaries had not been clearly defined. Through the 1960s and early 1970s, the growth in lodges and club lodges came mainly from Sydney people with some clubs emerging from regional NSW.

The final stage of the Thredbo Alpine Hotel was completed in 1967 and this released the resources to develop the Merritts area, adding some much-needed intermediate and learning areas to Thredbo's terrain mix.

To enhance the resort's summer offering, the golf course and tennis courts were built and there was even lawn bowls for a time on what is now the Village Green. Two T-bars were built on the central slopes and the Snowgums double chairlift was opened in 1980 – the fastest lift of its kind in Australia at the time.

Communal living in a club or commercial lodge had underpinned skiing and mountain resorts throughout Europe and certainly throughout Australia until the 1970s, when demand for apartment-style accommodation began to grow.

The interest in skiing grew alongside – the 1970s and 80s was an era of tremendous growth, stimulating the establishment of the Blue Cow resort on the Perisher Range and the expansion of the existing resorts there – Perisher Valley, Smiggin Holes and Guthega.

Thredbo felt the competition and was not doing as well as it might in the face of it, so in 1986 it engaged some North American experts – Group Delta and Farwell & Associates – to develop a skifields plan.

The plan called for $40 to $60 million in investment and involved summer slope grooming to create Australia's

first supertrails and at the same time allow skiing with minimal snow cover.

It also called for a dedicated beginner area close to the base of the mountain, the introduction of extensive snow-making and increased lift capacity.

Dusseldorp himself kept a very close interest in Thredbo and remained a frequent visitor, and while he recognised the need for another wave of development for Thredbo, he saw it was no longer something that suited Lend Lease. Kim Clifford, Kosciuszko Thredbo's current general manager was one of the people who helped develop that plan and recalled presenting it to the Lend Lease board.

'It was going to give Thredbo the lease of life it desperately needed and within a week or so they came back and said "it's a great presentation, but we've actually decided to sell the resort".'

But Dusseldorp wanted to know where it would go. 'He said, "I'd like to know who we are going to sell it to",' Albert van der Lee recalled. 'I think there were a couple of applicants who got the red light.'

The company that got the green light was Amalgamated Holdings Limited, an entertainment, hospitality and leisure business that included Rydge Hotels and Greater Union cinemas in its brands.

Like Dusseldorp, AHL's chairman Alan Rydge was not a skier. 'It certainly wasn't because I wanted to ski there, because I couldn't ski. As a board, we were looking for expansion opportunities but we didn't have a business plan to go and buy a ski resort.

'We were approached by Lend Lease to consider a position in Thredbo. They had their own reasons for doing that. Dick (Dusseldorp) was still very actively involved in an emotional sense as to what happened to the resort and from my indications, was very sensitive as to who should be given the opportunity to purchase it. For one reason or another, we fitted their criteria,' Rydge recalled.

'Lend Lease had done a lot of work with Group Delta preparing a plan for the resort's expansion ... basically it just came down to this question: "will you back snowmaking? Is it going to work or isn't it?"'

The evidence for Alan Rydge and his board was good enough – they backed the system and the overall development plan and took over in January 1987.

In their first few years at the resort, AHL invested around $60 million in Kosciuszko Thredbo, in snowmaking, the Friday Flat project and new lifts and village infrastructure. That underpinned expansion into areas like Woodridge and Crackenback Ridge and Riverside Cabins and other resort landmarks.

These are covered in the following chapters. On the following pages, there is also a glimpse of where the resort might head over its next phase of growth.

The 45-year head lease under which Kosciuszko Thredbo operates came into effect on June 29, 1962 and contained an option for a further 50-year lease.

On June 15, 2006, Kosciuszko Thredbo exercised its option with the next 50-year lease running from June 29, 2007.

Thredbo in 2057

How will Thredbo evolve over the next 50 years? Nothing will change its natural attributes – the river running through it, its uncanny orientation to the sun and the way the village gets the best of it but the slopes avoid its harshest winter angles or, for skiers and boarders, the extent of its vertical drop and the variety in its terrain.

But how will the village evolve and what will alter in the way the mountain is used?

'Look at that photograph of Sponar and Anton (page 11),' Kim Clifford said. 'There are two guys standing on a muddy track pointing up at the side of a hill and saying "one day that's going to be a ski resort" – look at where we are now.

'They believed Thredbo could become an internationally recognised resort, Dusseldorp believed that. But would any of them have foreseen exactly how it would emerge with technologies like snowmaking or high speed detachable chairlifts?'

Whatever the specific changes might be, both Clifford and architect Robin Dyke are convinced more environmentally friendly building and operating technologies will be in place.

That too, is part of an evolution. Thredbo has been using double-glazing since the mid 1980s, using the sun's energy in a passive way.

Thredbo has had dual flush toilets and shower savers for about 25 years – every new building or renovation had to include them.

In 1973 or 1974, Thredbo's sewage treatment plant treated about 1600 kilolitres a day with 2400 beds in the village. In 2006, with 4400 beds, the plant seldom treated in excess of 1300 kilolitres a day.

OPEN CANVAS: *This sketch map was retrieved from a collection of papers belonging to the late John Gam, an original Kosciuszko Thredbo shareholder (the papers were found at a Newcastle tip). The map was probably drawn shortly after the 1959 winter and even if some of its features – the airstrip for example – didn't eventuate, it did foresee others like the Merritts access chairlift.*

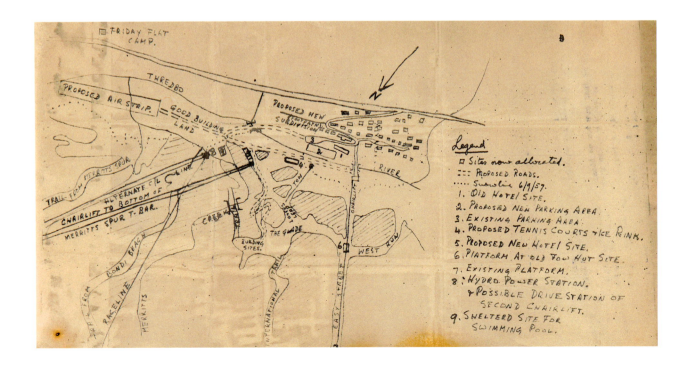

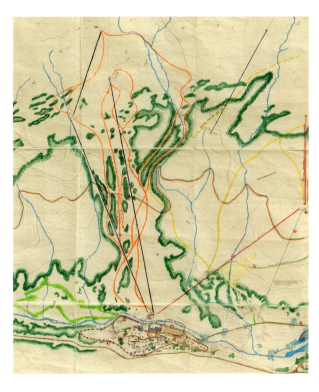

LANDMARKS: *The Lend Lease master plan prepared by Dick Dusseldorp, Albert van der Lee and others is seen here in its 1967 version. It was so well conceived, when a new master plan was developed in the mid-1990s, it was found to fundamentally match that original footprint.*

'Thredbo didn't introduce dual-flush toilets because of some law or regulation imposed on it, it was because it made sense, environmentally and commercially – if Lend Lease had to treat less water, they saved money. It made sense,' Clifford said.

Robin Dyke concurred. 'Kosciuszko Thredbo can make decisions without referring to a bureaucracy. It can respond almost instantaneously to changes in the commercial environment, to changes in technology and to changes in the needs and expectations of the guests.'

Major projects likely to be a part of the village's evolution include central facilities such as the Thredbo Alpine Hotel and Valley Terminal.

'They really haven't changed from the early days. They need upgrading, they really are past their use-by date,' Robin Dyke said.

There are numerous options. Removing the maintenance facilities from the Valley Terminal area and developing accommodation there is one option. Redeveloping the hotel on its existing site and opening up the Valley Terminal area for skiers and boarders is another.

It's all part of a process that accounts for local conditions but also draws on some of the best ideas from mountain resorts around the world.

'It's not one person's idea, not one company's idea – a lot of our stakeholders travel every year and bring back ideas from other resorts,' Clifford said.

He emphasises that Kosciuszko Thredbo is not the only investor in the village 'we probably represent about 30 per cent of the investment in the village overall, but it's a partnership. If we can improve our operations, that improves everyone's investment.'

The Village Centre will remain crucial in the evolution of the resort. 'We'll reinforce that at every opportunity,' Robin Dyke said. 'That urban precinct is really important to round off the experiences a guest has. It becomes a meeting place.'

It's the same wherever you go in the world, Kim Clifford said, 'Whether it's a 500-year-old village in the mountains of Europe or a 50-year-old village in Australia, the best of them just have one heart or centre, if you try and duplicate them, you detract from both.'

Technological and environmental change will also drive what happens on the mountain. Invention and innovation may bring self-propelled skis or more cloud seeding – they're the intangibles, the more certain changes will come in lifts, trail management and snow-making.

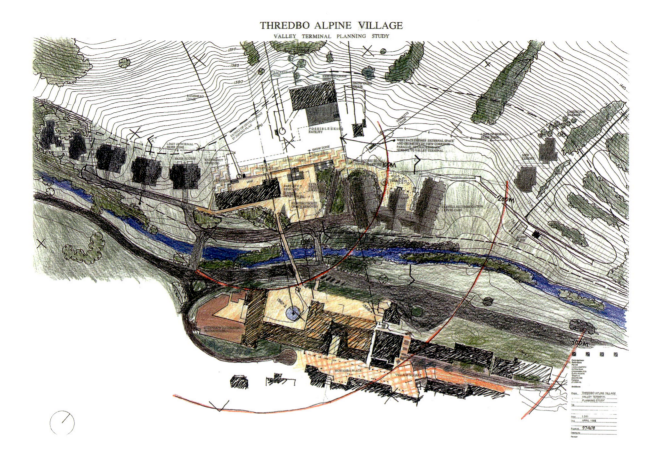

THREDBO ALPINE VILLAGE
VALLEY TERMINAL PLANNING STUDY

The first lift to be replaced could well be the Kosciuszko Express. 'We think we can probably get more certainty in windy conditions by replacing it with a heavy six-seater chair,' Kim Clifford said.

It is one of the best-used chairlifts in the world. 'It goes back to Dick Dusseldorp's principal for year-round operations. It would be very easy for us to just run things for peak periods, but we really have stuck to that principal of Dusseldorp's, that you have to stay open to get the visitors. 'We have opened a bar, restaurant, chairlift and hotel seven days a week, 365 days of the year, in many ways for the last 45 years.

'There's probably been 4 to 5 million summer tourists that have ridden that lift over the past 45-odd years,' Clifford said.

Apart from that lift, three other lines have been selected for further investigation. One is the Golf Course Bowl, with a lift running to the western side of Karels T-bar, 'on the natural ridgeline there where you sort of fall into the Dead Horse Gap area; that's well and truly within our lease area,' Clifford said.

MOVEMENT AT THE STATION: *One concept for Valley Terminal is to build a hotel next to the existing building on the car park and tennis courts and relocate the maintenance workshop. This plan incorporates dwellings along the bottom of the Crackenback Supertrail, on the western side of Valley Terminal.*

Another chairlift would use the top part of High Noon, above the steep of High Noon and head into the area to the east of the top of Antons T-bar.

The third lift is a T-bar to run in the area between the upper part of Sponars, an area called Fiveways, up to some of the high drift skiing – a similar line to Sponars, but probably 500m to the west, giving access back into the Basin area.

Snowmaking, and particularly the efficiency of the system, will receive attention. Thredbo has proven the success in its application and in many ways this has become the resort's insurance against the unknown perils of climate change.

The technology is changing, 'if you want to make snow on Pitt Street, you can, it's purely a matter of cost,' Kim Clifford said.

There could also be a balance between the energy requirements of the village and the snow-holding capability of the mountain.

'You could put pipe work under Friday Flat and use the heat exchange process to cool the earth and heat the village for instance,' Robin Dyke said.

'There are lots of those kinds of issues that haven't really been addressed, that would be prohibitive in today's dollars, but may become feasible.'

Following a run of winters with reliable natural snow cover, in 2006 all Australian alpine resorts suffered with marginal natural snowfall.

Nevertheless, Thredbo had a very successful 2006 season. 'A lot of that goes down to a $2 million investment in the automation of our snowmaking system,' Clifford said.

A further $2 million in snowmaking for the 2007 season gives Thredbo automated coverage on the steeper (eastern) side of High Noon, Playground on the Cruiser, the Racecourse off the Supertrail, the Village Trail, all the area from Sundowner to Friday Flat and also the area from Sundowner into Lovers Leap behind Valley Terminal.

The next 50 years of Thredbo will no doubt bring evolution at a greater pace than the last 50 years. Factors such as new building techniques, innovations in snowmaking and lifting technology and the input and ideas of Thredbo's customers, community and management will all play a part in shaping Thredbo in the year 2057.

MOUNTAINSIDE: *New and replacement lifts will be more efficient, improving access to existing terrain and better serving new terrain within the existing lease area. Increased capacity on the Kosciuszko Express and into the Golf Course Bowl are highlights of the plan.*

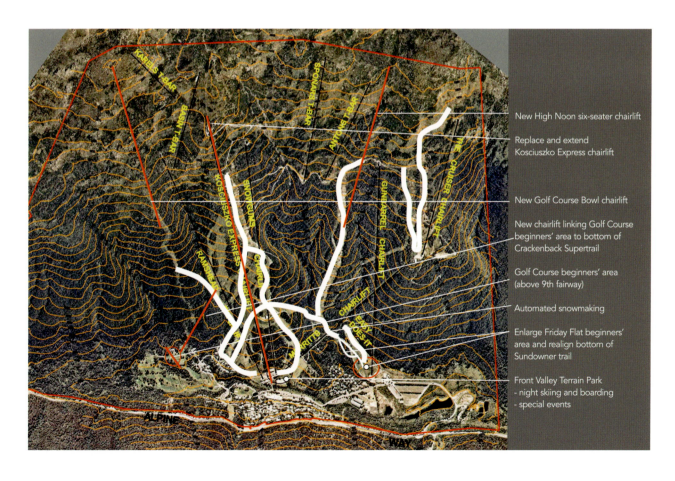

New High Noon six-seater chairlift

Replace and extend Kosciuszko Express chairlift

New Golf Course Bowl chairlift

New chairlift linking Golf Course beginners' area to bottom of Crackenback Supertrail

Golf Course beginners' area (above 9th fairway)

Automated snowmaking

Enlarge Friday Flat beginners' area and realign bottom of Sundowner trail

Front Valley Terrain Park
- night skiing and boarding
- special events

An Australian mountain village

The 1950s and 1960s was a stunning era for Australian architecture: stunningly uninspired, considering some of the housing and high-rise styles, but stunningly enlightened with accomplishment like the Sydney Opera House.

The Snowy Mountains Scheme was another grand endeavour of the era and it brought the workforce and the engineers and, with them, many of the ideas. Thredbo was an opportunity to express those ideas and aspirations, using platforms as simple as club lodges and pre-fabricated huts, and as complex as ski lodges that could straddle creeks. The village in the valley began to grow, crafted to complement its natural surroundings.

With the Kosciuszko Chairlift and Thredbo Hotel syndicate created in May 1955, the group had to generate some commercial interest in its venture. The chairlift and hotel might have been projects for the syndicate, but it needed clubs and business people to build and operate the lodges and underpin the broader village development.

Bill Bursill was one of a party that visited Thredbo in October 1955. Many of them had come from Sydney to Cooma by train.

'Sir William Hudson (SMA commissioner) organised a group of jeeps from the Snowy Mountains Authority to pick up all the people from the train and take them out to the site which was Friday Flat, where the SMA had the camp,' Bursill said.

They spent the night at the SMA camp and the next morning hiked around the area on one of the first site inspections; exploring the valley and slopes of what they were told would become a major ski resort.

'There were about 40 or 50 of us altogether from Sydney,

MOUNTAIN HUTS: Ramshead Hut on Diggings Terrace (above) is the only remaining Thredbo building based on portable buildings from Norway purchased by the Snowy Mountains Authority. Tussock (left) at Crackenback Ridge takes elements of that original form and reinterprets it.

businessmen, skiers, old skiers that wanted to see what could be done,' Bursill said. 'We talked about where the village should be.'

They settled on a location; Bursill doesn't think it was exactly where the village ended up, 'but it was pretty close to it.'

Within the syndicate there had been tension over the original village location, particularly the site for the hotel and the side of the river it would sit. Once that site was identified, it would create a centre from which the rest of the project could expand.

Syndicate members Geoffrey Hughes and Charles Anton, while working for the syndicate's progress, were also representing club interests. In Hughes' case, that meant finding a site for the Crackenback Ski Club, while Anton and the Ski Tourers' Association would build Roslyn Lodge and Kareela Hutte.

The village was being developed from a clean palate. Geoffrey Hughes recalled the hesitation over the site selection for the hotel, which in turn affected his club site. He said the syndicate originally wanted to put the hotel on the site of what is now the Village Green and its ponds.

'And I said, "Well, in that case, can I have this site?" They

lit up and thought they'd better have a look and then they said, "oh, this is much better, we'll have this site for the hotel – you can go back up the hill a bit".

'That was all right,' Hughes said. 'That's the way these things happen and we still got a very handy site for the Crackenback Ski Club.'

Constance Hughes Crisp, Geoffrey Hughes' sister, and Robert Maclurcan designed Crackenback. It was the first building in the village to get a roof. Work started in the summer of 1956-57 and it was ready for occupancy in winter 1957.

With the site for the hotel resolved, Eric Nicholls applied his town planning experience to create Thredbo's first subdivision.

Tony Sponar, who had been appointed area manager by the syndicate, was overseeing lift and infrastructure development and also pushing to fill some of the sites. He pursued Bill Bursill, who had indicated to Sponar during a visit to the Kosciuszko Chalet that he'd be interested in building a lodge if they got '… permission from the government to start something …' at Thredbo.

Bill Bursill had a successful business in the Campbelltown General Store supplying that district with farm supplies and the town with groceries – 'the old general country store that we had in those days.'

'Tony Sponar phoned to say that the land was picked and ready – he had picked one in the centre for me.'

Bursill was keen to get the lodge built but was busy enough with his store. Sponar kept the wheels turning, at various times letting Bursill know that he'd bulldozed the site and then letting him know that 'as the sewerage for the village is going past your block of land, I have dug your sewerage trench. So come up and finish the job.'

Eventually, Bursill did: 'I got two semi-trailers together and three campervans and made the trip down to Thredbo with all the building materials … and took the builders down.'

The village was growing – the syndicate had bought some huts from the Snowy Mountains Authority to create its lodge and sold one to the Ski Tourers' Association, which became Roslyn Lodge (named in honour of Roslyn Wesche who died in the Kunama disaster – see chapter two).

These huts had been imported by the SMA from Norway – they had good credentials for an alpine environment, having started life as shelter for the German Luftwaffe stationed in Norway during the Second World War. One remains – it is the basis of the Ramshead Ski Club on Diggings Terrace.

The huts were transported to Thredbo in stages, the final four were reconstructed to create The Lodge Hotel by a pair of Hungarians, Bela Racsko and Steve Szeloczky who went on to create the Sigma building company, and were

---

REACH FOR THE SKY: *Sastrugi (above right) on Diggings Terrace was designed and built in 1958 for Kosciuszko Thredbo's first chairman Thyne Reid, and his family, contributing to Thredbo's innovative style. Elevation (below), on the site of the former Lietelinna Lodge on Bobuck Lane carries on the tradition.*

behind the design and construction of numerous other Thredbo buildings.

The first commercial lodge to open for business was Candlelight, in 1958. It was built for Hungarian immigrants Suzanne and Kornel Deseo and operated by them for two decades.

Dick Dusseldorp described them as setting the standard: 'They were the best … they stayed the best as long as they had it.'

Another couple who made their mark at this time was Karel and Sasha Nekvapil.

Sasha Nekvapil and Tony Sponar were Czech national champions who represented Czechoslovakia at the 1948 St Moritz Winter Olympics.

Karel, Sasha, her brother Frank Prihoda and Sponar, used various means and paths to flee communist Czechoslovakia in the winter of 1948-49 and all ended up working together in St Anton.

With their experience in the mountains of Czechoslovakia, then Austria, and Sasha's status as a skier, the Nekvapils had the perfect credentials to run a ski lodge. They also had some local understanding, having worked as ski instructors at Mt Buller in Victoria in the early 1950s and later at Charlotte Pass.

They built Sasha's Lodge which opened for business in 1959 and was renamed the Black Bear Inn in 1971.

Bill Bursill's construction project 'ran from 1957 through to 1958 and probably 1959.'

He recalled the eight-bedroom lodge as snug and warm. 'Every wall was insulated with cork so you could virtually heat Bursill's Lodge with a candle.'

He leased the lodge to others to operate, so it was known for a time as Leo's Lodge when it was run by Leo Pockl until the name Bursill's Alpine Lodge eventually stuck.

After numerous renovations and additions, it is now the Denman.

From Cees Koeman's recollections, 'The way the village started, they were either club lodges or small businesses in the form of commercial lodges with mum in the kitchen and the father chopping wood and the kids helping in the lodge and so forth.

'You would have a genuine bed and breakfast situation and they were very successful and created a wonderful atmosphere in the village.'

Ann and Cees Koeman's lodge, Kasees, was Thredbo's first commercial apartment building. It was designed by Bela Racsko and built in 1965 by Cees Koeman.

AN AUSTRALIAN MOUNTAIN VILLAGE

In the context of the era, with the availability of resources and labour, Thredbo's growth was stunning, an indicator of the underlying demand. From a blank sheet in 1955, by winter 1958 there were 15 lodges built and by 1960 there were about 60.

When Lend Lease took over Kosciuszko Thredbo in 1961, the immediate objective was to improve the infrastructure, which in turn would underpin further village development. It also had to establish some boundaries.

In the early years, the layout of the lots could be hit and miss. A shortage of staff to supervise or survey and mark the sites, meant when clubs or commercial operators were granted a site to build, the footprint of that building might not necessarily match the layout of the lots on the subdivision map.

The Crackenback Castle site is an example. Originally built as Grayson, a lodge for local bus operator Gus Grayson and his wife Margaret, the Clive Lucas, Stapleton & Partners 1997 *Thredbo Alpine Village Conservation Plan*, notes it was believed 'Lend Lease were required to rearrange the allotments to accommodate this property.'

Albert van der Lee recalled one of his first tasks as Thredbo's resident engineer was to put the existing subdivisions in order – 'the boundaries had not been clearly defined in many cases and they had to be redefined because the buildings had happened without substantial reference to the boundaries.'

Infrastructure work in the summer of 1962-63 proceeded at a feverish pace and included a sewerage treatment plant – septic tanks were out – improvements to the water supply system and the provision of electricity. Before 1963, electricity was from generators.

Under the head lease model, Kosciuszko Thredbo was responsible for securing leases with its sub lessees but the Parks Trust and later the National Parks and Wildlife Service (NPWS), as the arm of the NSW Government, determined the nature of those leases.

'There were two types of sub-lease,' Albert van der Lee said, 'a commercial lease and a club lease … but in actual fact, there were three types of operation going on – commercial, club and private. About 12 or 15 buildings at the time were privately owned or operated.

'These people had to make a choice whether they went into a club lease or a commercial lease. Most signed a commercial lease because it gave them more flexibility.

'Even clubs that were constituted as a club didn't sign a club lease, a lot of those opted for the commercial lease – such as Redbank,' van der Lee recalled.

It wasn't until the 1970s that Lend Lease applied to the NPWS for a third type of lease, an apartment lease. They agreed to it, but under a number of conditions, the main one being to eliminate permanent residency in the village, other than for people who worked there.

CARAVANS IN THE SNOW: *Riverside Cabins were conceived to be compact and economical; to make property ownership in Thredbo available at a lower price but with well-designed buildings in a unique location. Riverside was built in four stages between 1991 and 1994.*

'The company, Lend Lease, didn't disagree with that at all,' van der Lee said. 'The last thing they wanted was to have Thredbo turn into a retirement village.'

Kasees was the first commercial apartment building in 1965, but the first block of strata-titled apartments in Thredbo was Bobuck, which was finished in 1969.

Renovations and redevelopments of club and commercial lodges occurred, as they still do, but many new buildings from this time were self-contained apartments – major projects like the Thredbo Alpine Apartments which replaced the staff lodge or on a smaller scale like Crackenback Castle or the ironically named Frankheinzstein's which was an amalgam of its three creators, Frank Prihoda, Heinz Reichinger and Helmut Steinoecker.

The village itself was filling out. Land was plentiful within the lease area but new directions had to be determined. While the main village was compact in its design, with buildings rubbing shoulders much as they might in a European setting, the aim for Woodridge Estate was to create a lower-density development.

Woodridge was planned in the 1980s and its first two stages built in the late 1980s and mid 1990s. Gentler slopes and more densely wooded terrain meant the mix of buildings in Woodridge – self-contained cabins and lodges, some bed and breakfasts and the River Inn at the edge – could sit comfortably among the snow gums.

It had humble origins, starting life as a caravan park and low-cost staff accommodation venue, but its style was in such demand, its first two stages were built out reasonably quickly, followed by the third stage, surrounding the Thredbo Leisure Centre.

SLOPESIDE: *Crackenback Ridge created the opportunity for ski-in/ski-out accommodation and to extend Thredbo's architectural style. One of its lodges, Tanglewood, has a 24m-long stone wall as its spine with multiple floor levels unfolding from it.*

Not everyone who wanted to buy in could afford Woodridge prices however, so the objective with Riverside Cabins was to broaden the appeal of Thredbo, to allow people to invest at a lower cost.

The inspiration for Riverside Cabins came from a very humble block of flats in Parallel Street, Falls Creek. The Mini Flats, as they are known, were built by Falls Creek lodge owner Ore Frueauf in the 1970s.

David Osborn, Thredbo's managing director in the 1990s, used to visit a friend, Jane Parker, one of the founders of the Country Road clothing label at her Mini Flat in Falls Creek.

'It was a low-cost entry to the market, it was barely big enough to have a kitchen but that didn't matter – they spent so little to buy it, they could afford to eat out every night.

'So that was my brief to (architect) Robin Dyke for Riverside,' David Osborn said – 'build us some caravans in the snow – compact and economical but well-designed.'

Developing low-cost, entry-level accommodation has proven success in the mountains, but the challenge is to create something with sustainable design and quality.

Consider the failure of some of the high-rises in the mountains of France that seduced aspirational Parisians in the 1970s and the Riverside project becomes all the more successful in contrast.

For this Thredbo project, Robin Dyke initially developed minimal plans and built models to show how the wet areas and kitchens would work. The nature of the site meant the best type of development would be lightweight, with pier-type foundations and floors suspended above the ground. One of the most ingenious aspects of Riverside was in the means of its construction.

Originally, frames and building materials were to be moved in by crane, but this proved difficult to manage. So the solution of the builder, John Fielding of Bellevarde Constructions, was to create a roadway out of scaffold, and the actual building footprint became the construction platform.

'When the project was completed and the builder removed the scaffolding, the surrounding vegetation was intact. It was as though the buildings had been dropped in by helicopter,' Robin Dyke recalled.

Riverside was built in four stages between 1991 and 1994 with the restaurant added in June 1995.

Planning for Crackenback Ridge started in the early 1990s with the subdivision and infrastructure work undertaken in 1993 and 1994. Woodridge and Riverside had helped improve the mix of accommodation, but one area Thredbo was lacking was in on-snow or true ski-in/ski-out accommodation – what the Americans call 'beachfront'.

Andrew Cocks, Kosciuszko Thredbo's resort engineer and then property development manager in the 1990s, spent a lot of time looking at the options.

'We actually went back and revisited some of the planning work Dusseldorp had done in the 1960s and that included a village up at Merritts Spur and a village in the Lover's Leap area. We looked at those again and tried to assess their feasibility and just how you'd run satellite villages like that.'

They eventually discarded the satellite village concept in favour of something on the fringe of the ski field.

'The Crackenback Ridge area always made sense,' Cocks said. But they struggled with access and their desire not to interfere with the golf course.

'Then while we were having a good look at it, we found there were a couple of routes that we would be able to open up, without disturbing the golf course too much, that would make access to that area reasonably easy.'

Crackenback Ridge changed the dynamics of accommodation within Thredbo. It provided different benchmarks and it has also inspired some stunning architecture.

CAMPS AND COMMERCE: *The lodge at the top left of the picture is Candlelight, Thredbo's first commercial lodge. It was built by Suzanne and Kornel Deseo who operated it for two decades. The caravan was typical of the era – builders and club members would use any accommodation they could find while working on their construction projects.*

The Thredbo style

Although it contains considerable diversity, Thredbo's architecture has a particular form and style, something Robin Dyke of Daryl Jackson Robin Dyke, Kosciuszko Thredbo's consulting architects, traces back to the Norwegian pre-fabricated huts purchased from the Snowy Mountains Authority.

That original style involved a building with a stone base, a robust material to help cope with being surrounded by snow at ground level and lightweight timber cladding above.

'It was quite rudimentary, but a lot of the club lodges looked like that. To dress them and give them an alpine character, the inclusion of stonework and the fairly common colour scheme of mission brown with white windows gave the village a bit of a look,' Dyke said.

The clubs and the commercial lodges were developing an architectural style, but it was in some of Thredbo's private developments that the architects of the era were expressing themselves.

Some significant Sydney architects were involved with Thredbo's early buildings, including Eric Nicholls and Otto Ernegg (Sastrugi), Harry Seidler (Lend Lease or Seidler Lodge) and Peter Muller (Wombiana).

According to Dyke, 'it was a case of the Sydney School meeting the parks' building code and that morphed into the Thredbo style.'

SEIDLER IN THE SNOW: *Seidler Lodge was Harry Seidler's interpretation of a European mountain lodge in a modern Australian setting. These photographs, by Max Dupain, from the State Library of NSW's Harry Seidler collection, were taken for Seidler's successful submission for the 1965 Wilkinson Award.*

CREEK CROSSING: *At its western side, Seidler Lodge actually straddles a small creek. Despite its unique design, it follows the form of Thredbo Village in its extensive use of stone and wood.*

In a 1998 interview with Helen Dalley on the Nine Network's *Sunday* program, Seidler, then aged 75, revealed he had been a skier since he was six. 'I've always loved skiing to this day. And to me it (the Thredbo ski lodge) was a real challenge, to try and make something that has the character and the atmosphere of these charming villages in Austria and other parts of Europe, but obviously translated into an idiom that's more part of our own time.'

The long, distinctive ramp that provides pedestrian access to Seidler Lodge, as it is now known, is a feature it shares with his famous Rose Seidler house, built in Wahroonga in 1950.

The lodge relates to its landscape in a stunning way, in part straddling a creek in the way Thyne Reid envisaged the hotel might straddle the Thredbo River.

In its 1997 *Conservation Plan* for Thredbo, Clive Lucas, Stapleton & Partners described Seidler Lodge as an 'excellent example of the Bush School architectural style.' The lodge won the prestigious Wilkinson Award for architecture in 1965.

The Conservation Plan also recognised Sastrugi as an excellent example of the 'abstract modernism' architectural style 'with a strong expressive quality.'

Sastrugi was designed by Eric Nicholls' firm Nicholls, Elliot and Nicholls, along with Otto Ernegg in 1958 for syndicate chairman Thyne Reid and his family.

It was an era when Sydney architects were starting to become more adventurous, stirred on by projects such as the Sydney Opera House and increasing international exposure. Thredbo, with its outstanding natural qualities, gave a rare environment for their expression.

Other landmark buildings in the late 1950s include Wombiana, which remains in largely original form. It was designed by Palm Beach architect Peter Muller (he also designed Obergurgl) and built for the Richardson family who had the Victa Lawn Mower Company (named for its founder Mervyn Victor Richardson).

Berghutte, completed in 1958, has had many alterations from the original design of Frenchs Forest architect Derek King, but most significant is the original A-frame that remains intact.

Given the European influence in Thredbo, and the large number of European migrants who settled there to build businesses or who became regular visitors in summer or winter, it wasn't surprising that buildings emerged in a European style – such as De Dacha which Albert van der Lee designed (along with the whimsical miniature Duck Dacha in the pond nearby).

However, as the NPWS developed its guidelines, the Austrian-themed building was actively discouraged by both the building code and Kosciuszko Thredbo – the company sought to enhance an indigenous style.

'The architectural character of the village was evolving from the simple mountain hut and Snowy demountables. Larger buildings like the Mowamba Apartments tried to move the style, tried to keep it going in a way,' Robin Dyke said.

With the construction of the new quad chair and its bottom station at Valley Terminal in 1990, the redevelopment of the precinct allowed Robin Dyke and his partner, landscape architect Jane Coleman, to create a link so the new and old buildings would stand side by side.

They recommended similar paint colours to those used on Friday Flat for the lift and maintenance buildings, a 'weathered grey' for the timber with a weathered copper Colorbond roof and a darker grey.

The more European style of Valley Terminal was acknowledged with a Venetian Red trim, but overall, the makeover significantly changed the image of the area.

'The next project was to repaint the mission brown hotel and a grey and green-grey scheme was prepared which subtly highlighted the simple skillion pavilion forms and window boxes of the building," Robin Dyke said.

'In developing the final colour scheme, we talked to a large paint company to get the right grey and they named it Thredbo Grey.'

Dyke said this became the basis of a fresh new look for the village, helping to promote and unite the new developments of lifts and snowmaking and the development opportunities that remained.

But you can't please all of the people all of the time. He recalled 'ever constructive comments at the time referring to the colour schemes as "battleship grey" or "drab green" but we were convinced that the outcome had the potential to move the village to another level.

'It was only paint but it was very effective at making the architectural forms recessive in the landscape while highlighting the best and more significant features of each building.'

SIGNATURES: *The tower on the western end of the Thredbo Alpine Hotel was part of its final stage, completed in 1967-68. It has become an architectural feature of Thredbo, repeated in the Information Centre and the fire station, among other buildings.*

THE CONNECTION: *The footbridge is another Thredbo icon. It was an improved link between the hotel and the mountain, designed by Civil & Civic's architectural team and completed in a timber-framed construction in the summer of 1963-64.*

By the mid 1990s, prospective developers were being issued with more formal guidelines, saying a range of 'simple but important things like curtain walls were not permitted and windows must appear as holes within walls.'

The palette of materials stipulated by the NPWS building code also ensured a continuity of architectural style. That style was taken up by Andrew Norbury of Melbourne architects Metier 3 in his design of first Tanglewood and then Tussock in Crackenback Ridge.

'What appealed to me about Thredbo was the village in the valley,' Norbury said. 'Aesthetically, I like the homogeneous nature of the village – it has some order to it.'

He took the material requirements and re-interpreted them in a dramatic way. With Tanglewood, which won a 1997 Royal Australian Institute of Architects' award, that meant creating a spine, a stone wall about 24m long and 11m high, with multiple floor levels unfolding from that spine.

Tussock sits on a site at the edge of Crackenback Ridge, high in the estate, almost touching the bush.

'The guidelines call for a certain amount of stone cladding, but I didn't want the stone to be a veneer, I wanted to be able to experience it,' Norbury said.

So Tussock has a sweeping, curving boomerang wall which is a metre thick – something like the shape of Parliament House in Canberra.

Almost two thirds of the building is underground, with a sculptural pavilion that sits in the field at the top and disappears into the landform.

In Thredbo's inner village, buildings of the scale and quality of Elevation in Bobuck Lane, a redevelopment of the Lietelinna (Little Lena) site shows something of the direction of redevelopment and infill work and the creative potential that lies within Thredbo's building guidelines.

It's the evolution of the Thredbo style.

The Thredbo Alpine Hotel

The first building in Thredbo to raise a roof was the Crackenback Ski Club, but it wasn't the first to get under way, that was the syndicate's building, The Lodge.

According to Tony Sponar, the first sod for it was, appropriately, turned by Neville and Dudley Pendergast, 'descendants of the families who had first settled the closest freehold land, "Penderlea", almost 100 years ago.' (Sponar, p153).

The Lodge was habitable for the winter of 1957 and housed Tony and Lizi Sponar and their daughter Louise and provided some commercial accommodation.

It grew after that first winter with the addition of the SMA's Norwegian prefabricated huts to create the 54-bed Thredbo Lodge Hotel. This practical but simple facility, to the east of the existing Thredbo Alpine Hotel, became staff quarters when Lend Lease took over Kosciuszko Thredbo and embarked on the four-stage construction of the Thredbo Alpine Hotel.

He took an interest in most aspects of Thredbo, but for Dick Dusseldorp, the hotel was of special significance.

'Duss was really passionate about the hotel, I think he saw it was a means of securing Thredbo's status,' Thredbo resident Michelle Reichinger said.

Stage one was a simple accommodation facility and concourse with shops, but it was nevertheless the commercial heart of the village that the syndicate had envisaged. That building became known as the Coach House Inn Hotel; the Coach House chain was outbid by Lend Lease to buy Kosciuszko Thredbo in 1961, but was appointed to run the hotel by Lend Lease just before the 1963 winter.

The second stage, built in the 1962-63 summer, filled in the area beneath stage one and included public facilities such as bars and restaurants.

It introduced a signature Thredbo feature; the stairs that go through the public part of the concourse, up from the Keller, past the Bistro and level out at the Schuss Bar.

In themselves the stairs are unremarkable, but the design of the banisters to so cunningly have pairs of skis slotted into them is a rarity in the mountains (although nobody had anticipated snowboards when they put them on the drawing board).

The footbridge was also built around this time, improving the link between the hotel and Valley Terminal – it also has become a Thredbo landmark, with its appealing timber-framed construction.

According to the Conservation Study, the bridge was designed to complement the construction of a broad terrace in front of the Thredbo Alpine Hotel, then under construction. The hotel was completed in its current form in 1967 for the 1968 winter, when the tower and a new accommodation wing that runs at right angles to the river and now contains the reception area were built.

The tower created a link between the old and new wings of the hotel and became the prominent architectural feature of the village, a kind of structural acknowledgement of the mountains above – it was created by architect Duncan Horne of Hely and Horne, Thredbo's consulting architects at the time.

'It's pointing at the top of Crackenback,' Thredbo's current architect Robin Dyke said. 'And it was something at the end of the street that could have banners on it – it could be lit up, could have things hanging off it.'

The form of that architectural feature has been repeated by Robin Dyke in the Information Centre and it also appears in various guises at the village entrance, on the fire station, even at the bottom of the stairs that lead up to Friday Flat.

'I thought it was important to replicate that tower form in the Information Centre because it was a key arrival point. It's much more prominent being down on the road and it's an element that I think if you produce one there, you produce one somewhere else and maybe one pops up somewhere else, they become recognisable icons.'

The external structure of the hotel hasn't really altered since 1967, although the complex has changed substantially inside.

The original Piano Bar, now the Lounge Bar with its unique sunken bar, was always an important venue; a venue that stayed open late and would be the meeting point, a place for reunions and Friday night arrivals from Sydney and beyond.

It had a major makeover in 1993 and, while it was completely stripped out, much of the character of the original lounge remained.

Unfortunately, in 2000 some guests stoked up the open fire in the Lounge Bar a little enthusiastically before they went to bed. The fire that resulted was confined to the

THE CENTRE: The village grows and the Thredbo Alpine Hotel takes shape. It was built in three stages. The original lodge can be seen immediately above the hotel in the photograph at left.

suites at the front, but this required a further upgrade to the area and the open fire was replaced.

The Schuss Bar, an après-ski favourite on the upper level of the concourse has also been reconfigured – the bar originally stretched along in front of what is one of the best views in Thredbo of the Crackenback slopes.

The bar has been moved to the back of the room, opening the outlook for guests.

In 1994 a major restaurant renovation turned what was the Stuble into Segretto, and the Tom Groggin room became Cascades.

'Apart from transforming each space, these projects opened up the restaurant facilities to the central staircase that everybody walked through to the lifts.

'Similarly, the facilities were on show when guests had finished skiing and were walking past,' Robin Dyke said.

Other important additions to the hotel complex include the conference centre, completed in 1984, an essential asset for Thredbo's year-round viability and the Information Centre, added in 1994.

Mountain shelter

Once the syndicate built the chairlift, Charles Anton and his Ski Tourers' Association had the means to move the materials they needed for their mountain hut.

Building accommodation in the alpine zone was nothing new for the STA, after all, it had built Kunama Hutte and Lake Albina Ski Lodge.

The site for Kareela was chosen partly for convenience – it was right by what was initially the chairlift top station – and partly as the springboard for what some thought could become another village in Thredbo, although this never eventuated. Kosciuszko Thredbo eventually bought Kareela

---

SHELTER: *Eagles Nest, which has expanded over the years, originally housed the unloading area and top bullwheel of the Crackenback double chairlift. Despite its location and the severe weather it can encounter, the snow drifts away from the access zone. Here skier Chris Mader entertains the crowd as he drops in over a drift.*

from the STA in 1962 and it was then transformed into a day lodge, eventually becoming the restaurant it is today (see chapter three for more on Kareela).

A young Cees Koeman had his first job in Thredbo at Kareela. He arrived in the resort on Australia Day 1960, helped finish building the hut and spent winter 1960 there as hut manager. 'We were allowed to use the lift on a Saturday night. The engineer would start the lift for us and we would go down to the village and have some fun.

'He would start the lift again to send us back up at midnight sharp, but I wasn't always ready to go home, so a few times I had to walk back up in the middle of the night.'

It would have been a sobering walk.

The mountain environment makes unique demands on structures, even near the bottom of the valley. They are more severe at altitudes such as Kareela's (1646m) but even that pales in comparison with the almost polar pounding that a building with the exposure of Eagles Nest (1925m) has to endure.

Eagles Nest started life as the unloading station for the extended Crackenback double chair (the bullwheel actually remains within the building, inside the restaurant – not so much as a museum piece, it's just a bit hard to shift from this height).

From some angles, Eagles Nest might appear little more than

a sophisticated shed, but its function and endurance in its location is testament to its design and engineering.

Like Valley Terminal, the footbridge and the first and second stages of the Thredbo Alpine Hotel, Eagles Nest was designed by Civil & Civic's internal design department, with architect Peter Storey part of that team.

'The form (of Eagles Nest) is pretty smart,' in Robin Dyke's observation. 'Sitting on those rocks, I think the engineers that designed it did a terrific job in making that thing just perch there,' he admired 'the way it sits to the prevailing wind and the snow just blows straight off the roof.'

When the Crackenback double chair was replaced by the quad chair, with its own unloading platform outside Eagles Nest, the annexe was added to the side.

This was designed by Robin Dyke and made big enough for an oversnow machine such as a Kassbohrer to shelter inside. A large wind deflector once featured on Eagle's Nest's eastern side – it was there to help direct drifting snow away from the front of the building – but this has since been removed.

Near the bottom of the Kosciuszko Express lift, Valley Terminal might occasionally frustrate the people who bump their heads on its low-pitched ceilings as they work in it, but it is another building with a generous history.

Millions of people have passed through it to reach Australia's summit via the Kosciuszko Express and the Crackenback lift that preceded it. It housed generators and still houses quirky underground storage areas and important maintenance facilities.

In many ways, because it houses the offices of Kosciuszko Thredbo, it is the beating heart of the resort. But it is also the alpine heart of Thredbo, the place where the diehard skiers and boarders rub shoulders and express and explore their pursuit. Once upon a time they would rent a locker at Fleets and embark on their mountain adventure from that ski-hire/ski-shop. Now they'll contemplate the runs over a coffee at Avalanche Café, get a tune from Ronnie Duncan in his ski workshop, pick up a pair of demo skis from Rossignol in one direction or Salomon in another; maybe even sort out some problems at the medical centre.

The area held the first lift station when the Crackenback Chairlift was built in 1957-58, but the first part of Valley Terminal doesn't seem to have gone up until 1960.

It was added to in various stages during the 1960s, when it housed a ski hire, ski school and ski patrol facilities, a staff dormitory, a restaurant, bar and entertainment area. It first contained a surgery in 1967 in part of what was formerly a workshop area. The ticket office and eastern extension was built in 1981.

Getting a rubbishing

Because it holds the head lease, Kosciuszko Thredbo is responsible for all village infrastructure and most services, including roads, rubbish, water, public parking, snow clearing and signage.

This has extended its engineering skills and is a major, ongoing operation, but much of this work is unseen.

Right up until the early 1990s, Thredbo had a tip near its entrance. David Osborn, a keen white water canoeist, recalled canoeing the Thredbo River between the village and Jindabyne, probably in 1992. 'I saw some plastic bags had blown in from the Thredbo tip. I was appalled and felt personally responsible and said, "What modern resort still has a tip – and at its entrance?"

'So I organised to have it closed, but then KT had to spend about $50,000 a year on studies for the National Park and the Snowy River Shire while they cogitated over where the rubbish could go.

'We were getting nowhere, so I rang up the shire engineer at Corryong in Victoria and asked them if they would take our rubbish.'

The reply was direct and positive – the engineer told Osborn they'd love to have Thredbo's rubbish, '… we will never fill our tip and we could use the contribution.'

Osborn advised the NPWS 'they said, "you can't do that, you can't send your rubbish interstate. We will tell you where you have to dispose of it."

'So I sat down and wrote them a letter, remembering my first year in law I quoted Section 92 of the Constitution, which states that trade between states "shall be absolutely free."

'I never heard from them again about that.'

All the recyclables are separated out (about 50% of the waste stream in Thredbo is empty bottles and cans – skiers know how to party) and the remaining rubbish is compacted and baled and sent to Corryong in Victoria's Towong Shire.

Good sports

A sports centre had been part of the plan for Thredbo for decades – it was seen as an asset that could cement the resort's year-round appeal.

It came closer to reality in the early 1990s when Kosciuszko Thredbo, with renewed energy for summer business, recognised there were four core features it could offer – recreation, education, health and sport.

Rob de Castella, an Australian and Commonwealth marathon champion was director of the Australian Institute of Sport (AIS), the high-performance centre for the Australian Sports Commission at the time.

De Castella and the AIS had been approached by different resorts at different times to establish an AIS training centre. He was very keen on the idea – "I had trained at altitude at Falls Creek, Perisher and Thredbo. You can escape the hot summer climate and there are physiological advantages to training at altitude," de Castella said.

"We looked at a number of resorts, including Charlotte Pass and Mt Buller, but Thredbo was very pro-active, very committed and very enthusiastic to actually make it happen," de Castella said.

The proximity to Canberra (where the AIS has its main

STAY AND PLAY: *The Thredbo Leisure Centre was created to give elite athletes the opportunity for altitude training in a camp environment and improve the resort's range of facilities. Narelle Dower scales the indoor climbing wall (right) while Brett Thomas (below left) stretches out in the pool's 50m lanes.*

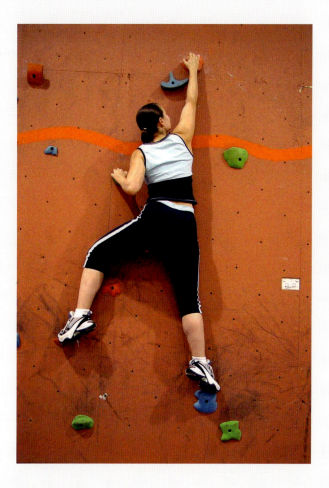

base) was also a bonus – it's a relatively short drive from Canberra but the travel to a Victorian resort would have been much more complex.

Rob de Castella, Dick Telford (the AIS performance coach) Don Talbot (from Australian Swimming) and Jim Ferguson, the director of the Australia Sports Commission, were invited to Thredbo and agreed to support the building of a sports centre at the resort.

The facility was built in 1995. The AIS contributed the naming rights and undertook to buy 5000 room nights a year in the Thredbo Alpine Hotel over a five-year period. The appeal for coaches and athletes was twofold – they had access to training at altitude, but they could also train as a group in a camp environment with all the intensive focus that offers.

The basketball courts and the gymnasium and the strengthening and conditioning equipment was very much a way of supporting the elite athlete program, but the broader appeal of what has become known as the Thredbo Leisure Centre was general recreation for the village and its visitors.

'That's why it has the water slide,' David Osborn said. 'In summer, families are such a big market, but what do you do when it's raining – and it does rain in the mountains – the pool is a fail-safe thing.

'So from our point of view, it was contributing to what we could offer in summer and it was also in the middle of a pretty crummy car park which is now Woodridge Stage 3, so it actually added value to that car park.'

Looking at it from the board table, guaranteed bed nights were a good way to underpin business and bring people into the village, but the Thredbo Alpine Hotel wasn't always so sure.

'I remember Anthony Cleary, the hotel general manager, coming to me,' Osborn said.

'We had a rugby team coming down the next week and they'd all just been fined for some outrageous display at the cricket.

'They were all coming to Thredbo and Anthony was saying to me "what are you doing, they're going to tear the place apart!"

'As it turned out, the cricket incident meant they were on their very best behaviour – there was never going to be a problem.'

But there were problems in the kitchen. When swimmer Michael Klim sat down to a breakfast of 28 Weet Bix, Cleary would ask Osborn how he was expected to make money on that. 'But then the next one to come along would be a gymnast who'd eat two bits of lettuce – it all averaged out in the long run.'

Swimmers loved the facility, particularly for the softness of the water – because it is sourced so high in the catchment, it is almost pure rain water which swimmers really enjoy swimming in.

The AIS bed night commitment has been consumed, however the naming rights remain and Thredbo now markets directly to the various sports and their teams.

On the mountain

2

Thredbo's lift and trail development was a pioneering opportunity. By the mid-1950s, skiing was patronised well enough to have bred a core of enthusiasts, so much so that supply was nowhere near matching demand. Accommodation was a bet in a ballot and lifts were sparse. Even if a skier could get into the mountains, there were few runs. Imagine the opportunity in an entire resort, a clean canvas. Especially when you can stand on one side of the valley and paint the canvas with the lifts and trails of your dreams as you look at the other side.

In Australian ski resorts, the typical progression was to build rope tows, then T-bars or Pomas, then chairlifts. This best fitted the resources available and meant the earlier, less capital-intensive lifts could quickly make a contribution towards those that would replace them.

It also followed a pattern of invention. Chairlifts and more sophisticated drag lifts such as T-bars and Pomas really only started to supersede rope tows in the late 1950s.

Even though Thredbo aspired to a different direction from the outset, reflected in the syndicate's business name – the Kosciuszko Chairlift and Thredbo Hotel – it was a rope tow that provided the first uphill transport.

Tony Sponar later wrote that he had wanted to open with the showpiece: 'I watched as an old piece of machinery was installed way up the hill to serve as an outdated rope tow. This was a waste of money and effort and gave a distorted picture about what the valley could offer.' (Sponar, p151).

But, as investors in a fledgling enterprise, his colleagues could be forgiven for wanting some cash. Besides, the years filter memories in all sorts of ways. In a memo to the syndicate dated April 16, 1957 and signed by Tony Sponar, he actually wrote:

'Last Sunday Geoffrey (Hughes) came forward with the proposal to put the (rope) tow in the new chairlift line. This arrangement, if realised, would in my opinion solve dozens of mutual problems.

'The greatest advantages I could see would be that the tow would become a business proposition and that the tow as it stands would, when we start erecting the chairlift, become 70% of the auxiliary rope way. For these and other reasons I would strongly support this proposal …' (THS collection – John Gam papers).

That first lift at Thredbo, the Crackenback rope tow, came with a rich, if tragic heritage. In the early 1950s, the Ski Tourers' Association had built Kunama Hutte in the Kunama Basin, beneath the dramatic slopes of Mt Northcote and Mt Clarke.

The terrain was steep enough to provide a course for the STA's Golden Eagle – a precursor of speed skiing as it is known today.

The first runner was Tony Sponar who is said to have hit a top speed of 129 km/h in his schuss on a course with a 250m vertical drop over its 800m length. To reach the Golden Eagle

OPEN FOR BUSINESS: *Winter 1957 and there are no easy rides on the Crackenback rope tow, but it's better than walking and it means the resort can host the NSW State Championships that year.*

standard, skiers had to complete the course in 42 seconds or less (35 or less for an instructor like Sponar).

As well as Sponar, there was a core of Thredbo pioneers among those who achieved Golden Eagle status, including Charles Anton, Geoffrey Hughes and Tommy Tomasi (Walkom, p100).

Tragedy hit in July 1956 however, when an avalanche destroyed Kunama Hutte, killing Roslyn Wesche but sparing the 11 other inhabitants.

The STA also had a rope tow at Kunama and only a few weeks after the avalanche, the tow hut was destroyed in a

BUSH MECHANICS: *To build the rope tow, materials were transported by flying fox – a single span of wire rope from the site of the Thredbo Alpine Hotel to the top of the first steep pitch on the lift line.*

fire stirred on by the fuel and gelignite kept in that building. 'We finished up with a heap of twisted iron, a rope going up and down the mountain with two singed ends and a whole lot of pulleys on the mountain,' Geoffrey Hughes said.

The events compounded to rip the heart out of the STA's Kunama Basin venture, but left enough equipment for the humble beginnings of Thredbo's first tow.

During the summer of 1955-56, the Thredbo syndicate had contracted to have a lift track cleared up towards what would become Kareela station.

This line was abandoned as it lacked flat terrain at its base and, after the 1956 winter, the combined efforts of enthusiasts who volunteered their labour because they simply wanted to get skiing going at Thredbo and a company called Ski Tows Pty Ltd cut a new line along the same lift line the Kosciuszko Express now follows. They built the rope tow, at a cost of £1870, using new components and those that could be salvaged from Kunama.

In winter 1957, Thredbo skiers were riding the tow from a launching point near Lovers Leap to Kareela, a distance of roughly half a mile (almost a kilometre).

On the mountain, there would be no looking back. Thredbo was able to fulfill its commitment to host the 1957 NSW Championships. It was on the skiing map.

After the 1957 winter, work was under way for the Crackenback double chairlift, to a design of the Swiss aerial lift pioneers, GMD Mueller.

The construction of the Crackenback chairlift was one of the first projects of a business founded by two Italian engineers, Franco Belgiorno-Nettis and Carlo Salteri. Their company, Transfield, would become a major Australian success in engineering and construction.

The Crackenback chairlift was formally opened on July 20, 1958 with its bottom station, close to where Valley Terminal is now, following the rope tow line and matching its top station. It was enough to keep driving the enthusiasm for development in Thredbo Village, but it still fell short of the newly formed company, Kosciuszko Thredbo's commitment to a 'chairlift one mile long' if it was to secure its head lease.

DRIVE AND INITIATIVE: *Volunteers from the Crackenback Ski Club with the rope tow drive unit, Easter 1956. They devised a system for the unit to haul itself over the river (and its suspension bridge) and up the slope to the site of the rope tow's bottom station.*

The original Crackenback rope tow was moved. It first became an extension of the chairlift line and then was taken across the mountain to have its bottom station near the current Black Sallees restaurant, roughly the top station of the existing Snowgums chairlift , but according to Albert van der Lee, it operated infrequently.

It was located there, he said, 'because there was a bit of a flattish hollow – for a rope tow you need a hollow sort of contour because the rope sags.

'It had been put there but it hadn't operated when I got there in 1962. The terrain there was very, very rough … you needed an enormous amount of snow. It operated a little bit in the first season I was there, 1963, but only for a few days.'

Stretched for finance, Thredbo's founding syndicate sold out to Lend Lease late in 1961 and the change was dramatic and immediate.

The Crackenback chairlift was extended to its current summit – Eagles Nest – for the 1962 winter and a T-bar was installed on what were known as the middle slopes, in the area where the grooming machinery is now housed, near Lovers Leap Station.

In the years that followed, lift development had two important influences – the need to access Thredbo's higher ground for reliable snow cover and the desire to provide skiing on some of the mountain's more challenging terrain.

After all, this was a motivating factor in Thredbo's development – to give those enthusiasts who had cut their teeth at Charlotte Pass, then challenged themselves on slopes such as Northcote, some invigorating vertical.

The Ramshead double chairlift and Basin T-bar opened for the 1963 season and, although totally overhauled as maintenance demands, they stand close to their original state today.

Ramshead had a slightly difficult birth. The top station was located in a hole and according to Cees Koeman, the mountain manager at the time, this was at the insistence of Dick Dusseldorp who wanted it out of the wind.

'He was very concerned about wind stoppages, so they built, at great cost, the top station inside this hole and of course, you can imagine what happened.

TAKE A SEAT: *Thyne Reid, the chairman of Kosciuszko Thredbo, and Dawn Hughes, an original shareholder, take their first ride on the Crackenback chairlift (right), in July 1958.*

DEADLINES: *A maintenance crew (below) endures the mountain weather to splice a new cable on the Crackenback double chairlift in 1963. The first stage of the hotel can be seen behind the Valley Terminal building.*

'In winter it filled up and the top station disappeared and you couldn't run the lift. It was moved some years later, up into a different spot,' Koeman said.

Some heavy snow years followed, in particular 1964 when Koeman said there was such depth in the snow, at one time all the lifts in Australia were snowed under and inoperable. 'We managed to keep the Crackenback lift open with the help of volunteers. We went on to the public address system asking for volunteers to help shovel and to shovel day and night. It was incredible.

'After a full day's work I would come and walk into the bistro area of the hotel there and sort out some volunteers amongst my boys who would go up the mountain and spend all night up there … my back still aches from 1964.

'I had a Holden ute at that stage and it disappeared completely in the valley. I walked over the top of it and in the spring, it finally showed its head.'

As the 1960s progressed and the sport showed steady growth, the demand for learning and what we today know as cruising terrain grew at Thredbo.

The ideal location for novices and improving skiers is to be at the mountain's base, but without such a thing as snowmaking to underpin the reliability of snow cover, Thredbo had to look to its upper slopes.

GAINING ALTITUDE: *The Basin T-bar was installed in 1962 to access more reliable snow on the upper mountain. It also formed a natural connection with the Ramshead and Crackenback chairlifts.*

The Merritts area was identified for this kind of terrain and reliable snow cover. Cees Koeman recalled '… looking for a gradient of slope that would satisfy and not scare the pants off the beginners and intermediates.'

They did a lot of scrub bashing through the Merritts area and eventually put a line in for double T-bars.

Merritts was a big investment for Kosciuszko Thredbo. In the early years of Lend Lease's ownership, Dick Dusseldorp and Albert van der Lee had walked the entire area over and over and consulted with experts including their Austrian ski school director Leonard Erharter to create a Thredbo master plan.

This involved the staged development of the hotel and an eastern subdivision. There was only so much work they could accomplish in a single summer construction season, so it wasn't until the company finished work on the

Thredbo Alpine Hotel, in 1967, that it was able to focus on the mountain and Merritts Spur.

Albert van der Lee saw Merritts as a major improvement in balancing Thredbo's terrain offering in an area of reliable snow cover, but it came with a weakness: its dependence on the slow and initially unreliable access from the Merritts double chairlift. 'It had some problems early on. One season it broke down and had a problem with the gearbox or something and people got very, very irate.'

EXPANSION: *The Merritts area was open to skiers in the 1968 winter. The Merritts double chairlift (in construction above left) made for a long ride but it was essential to access reliable snow cover on less intimidating terrain in the days before snowmaking. Duplex T-bars ran from the lift hut, while the original Merritts complex also included ski school and kiosk facilities.*

At the same time as the access chairlift, the duplex T-bars and Ski School T-bar were installed at Merritts, creating a new ski area for Thredbo.

A decade later, some beginner rope tows were installed at Merritts to make the learning process simpler, but until the Friday Flat development in the late 1980s, Merritts gave unbroken service as a nursery and improvers' area.

With village development and infrastructure the focus, it was almost 10 years before the lift-builders were back on the mountain. When they did return, the location of the new lifts was again ruled by the natural realities – snow cover on the lower mountain was simply too unreliable.

At the same time, the tough weather the upper mountain could face was such that the lifts had to remain low to the ground to be consistently operable. It was T-bar time.

In 1977 Antons T-bar and then in 1979 Sponars T-bar were built on the Central Spur area.

Karels T-bar was also built in 1979, above the Basin, giving Thredbo Australia's highest lifted point (2037m) and planting the seeds for the supertrails that would come later. Karels also improved access for that easy, delightful Thredbo adventure – the run to Dead Horse Gap.

In 1980, the Snowgums double chairlift opened, built to increase the lifting capacity from Valley Terminal and improve access to the Crackenback slopes.

Its top station was located low enough to give shelter from the worst of the wind but high enough for skiers to reach Sponars and Antons T-bars.

Then, in the mid 1980s, the technological revolution arrived. Snowmaking improved to the point where top-to-bottom skiing was a reliable option and the development of high-speed, high-capacity chairlifts meant skiers could get up the mountain with unprecedented efficiency.

With Amalgamated Holdings Limited as its new owners, Kosciuszko Thredbo had immediate access to resources for investment.

EASY GOING: *With snowmaking secured, Thredbo was able to create the dedicated Friday Flat beginner area at the base of the mountain. It also created a launching point for day visitors.*

In the summer of 1987-88, around $60 million was spent on the Friday Flat complex – the preparation of its beginner slopes, the base buildings and its Easy Does It quad chairlift – along with the Gunbarrel Express detachable quad chairlift and snowmaking infrastructure to cover the terrain those lifts accessed.

Friday Flat was part of a master plan review that Lend Lease had commissioned from a group including North American consultants Group Delta and Farwell and Associates before it sold its interests in the resort to Amalgamated Holdings Limited.

Completing the initial overhaul, the Crackenback double chairlift was replaced with a detachable quad in 1990 and the Merritts duplex T-bars were superseded by the Cruiser detachable quad chairlift in 1995.

To indicate the kind of impact technology can have on the mountain, consider the numbers. In 1989, on the

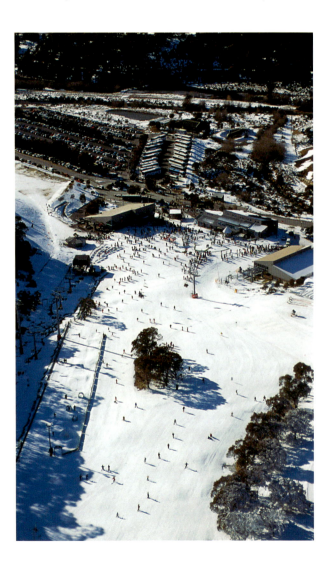

Crackenback slopes, the Snowgums chairlift could carry 1200 skiers an hour and the Crackenback chairlift 600 an hour – a total capacity of 1800 an hour (leaving aside the Ramshead chairlift with its different destination).

All of a sudden, with the installation of the Crackenback quad detachable chairlift , now known as the Kosciuszko Express, that capacity leapt to 4400 people. That's a lot more rides up the hill, but all those extra riders had to come down in some way.

The impact on trail use was dramatic. The response was to assert Thredbo's natural assets.

LIFT FOR THE LIFTS: *Helicopters were used from the early days. The smaller machine (below) was used to move sand, cement and other materials in the 1957-58 construction of the Crackenback double chairlift. By 1995, the Russian giant (above) could lift the lift towers into position for the Cruiser detachable quad chairlift.*

Lift chronology

AT THE GATE: *The ticket checking station at Valley Terminal – built in the style of its era (the 1960s) and boasting a healthy cover of snow.*

Dates refer to the first and, where applicable, last winter of operation.

1957 – 1958	Crackenback rope tow, from Lovers Leap to Kareela.
1958 – 1961	Crackenback double chairlift from Valley Terminal to Kareela.
1958 – 1963	Crackenback rope tow relocated first to run as an extension of the Crackenback chairlift and then to have its bottom station in an area near Black Sallees, the current top station of the Snowgums chairlift.
1962 – 1990	Crackenback double chairlift extended from Valley Terminal to Eagles Nest, (the existing Kosciuszko Express top station).
1962 – 1967	Middle T-bar, from Lovers Leap to what is now the Bunny Walk mid-station on the Snowgums chairlift (then relocated to Merritts and renamed the Ski School T-bar and then the Easy Rider T-bar).
1963 –	Basin T-bar.
1963 –	Ramshead double chairlift.
1964 – 1967	Crackenback rope tow relocated and shortened to run from Valley Terminal, a short way up the slope between the existing Kosciuszko Express and Ramshead lift lines.
1968 –	Merritts double chairlift.
1968 – 1995	Merritts duplex T-bars.
1968 – 1995	Merritts Ski School T-bar.
1977 –	Antons T-bar.
1978 – 1995	Harusch rope tows, beginner tows at Merritts and near Valley Terminal.
1979 –	Karels T-bar.
1979 –	Sponars T-bar.
1980 –	Snowgums double chairlift.
1988 –	Gunbarrel Express detachable quad chairlift.
1988 –	Easy Does It quad chairlift.
1990 –	Kosciuszko Express detachable quad chairlift (named the Crackenback Express until 2001).
1995 –	Cruiser quad detachable chairlift.
1995 –	Merritts Ski School T-bar shortened and renamed the Easy Rider T-bar.
2000 –	Friday Flat Snowrunner snow carpets.

Ski fashions

IN FASHION: *Snow sports have always been an opportunity for fashion designers. An early expression was in Paul Reader's Sydney Store (below left) in 1956. As the waterproofing and windproofing of fabrics improved, so did the function of the garments with Thredbo Racing Club members Ross Taylor (left) Guy Stephens and Tim du Temple showing their style in 1984. The progression into the 21st Century has seen lighter, more effective and versatile skiwear as worn by Jay Kelly in 2006 (below).*

The trail network

Lifts are simple to track and trace, but ski trails have a very different origin – some are carefully planned and neatly cut, some emerge in the chaos of events such as wildfire, some are trails blazed by pioneers and enthusiasts and a few just appear naturally.

In relative terms, skiing remained a pursuit with a pioneering edge through the 1950s, 60s and 70s, with long lift queues, basic equipment and rough going on mogul-studded slopes. There was no shortage of enjoyment – if there were a measure of pleasure, the reading would have been as high then as it is now – but as a tourist enterprise, the snow had a way to go.

Many factors conspired to push it along in the 1980s – among them was the competition between Australian alpine resorts and other tourist resorts, competition from New Zealand as a destination for skiers and the influence of the sophistication in North American destination resorts and the aspiration of Australian resort operators to match that.

Thredbo sought to put its mountain in balance and assert its status; the foundation for this was the revised master plan developed with the assistance of North American specialists Ted Farwell of Farwell & Associates and Jeff White of Group Delta.

Kosciuszko Thredbo's marketing director and then managing director in the 1980s, Wayne Kirkpatrick, said: 'The whole concept was about having the place in balance. You have a population of village residents and day visitors, you find out what that adds up to and then the lifting capacity, slope capacity, number of restaurants, car parks and so on.

'We developed a plan that involved the supertrail concept, (summer) slope grooming so you could ski with minimal snow cover, snowmaking and improved lifting capacity.'

Lend Lease recognised the merits of the plan and the scale of the investment required; it also recognised that it was moving in different directions. When Lend Lease embarked on the sale process for Thredbo, the master plan became part of it and Amalgamated Holdings Limited went about implementing it.

One of the crucial factors was to improve Thredbo's offering for beginner skiers.

As AHL chairman Alan Rydge explained: 'Before we built Friday Flat, we knew we weren't a great resort for beginners. I knew it because I learnt to ski there! 'Our research also highlighted the reality that if you can capture the beginner market and deliver a good quality product to them, you'll have them for the rest of their skiing life.'

Friday Flat was ideal because of its gentle terrain and because beginners could get straight on to the snow without riding a lift. It was all made possible by snowmaking, which could guarantee consistent coverage.

It also created a second entry point for the mountain, lessening the pressure on Valley Terminal with Valley Terminal serving resident skiers and Friday Flat day visitors.

The Gunbarrel Express chairlift also made sense of this, as it gave direct access to the Central Spur and a simple link to Merritts; the High Noon Supertrail was another card in a very strong hand.

'That's when we started to build the slopes called supertrails,' mountain manager Werner Siegenthaler said. 'High Noon from Gunbarrel and the Crackenback Supertrail – big wide trails.'

Another part of the strategy has been a reforestation program – around 20,000 snow gums planted to break up the runs.

'What we're doing here,' Siegenthaler said, 'is improving the environment but also making a greater variety of trails. We haven't made the Supertrails narrower, what we're doing is reforesting the mountain.

'It also helps your snow drifting and creates shade from the sun so your snow retention is better and it slows the wind down so it doesn't get blown from the top to the bottom or into Jindabyne.

'They are reasonably slow growing, but the trees we are planting here are all from seed that's been harvested in this area – so they should be used to these kind of conditions. They get propagated and we put them into the ground after they have got a start.'

The higher you go, the slower they grow, but around the 1400 to 1500m level, within five years there is a reasonable windbreak.

In the early days, Thredbo's ski runs were sometimes planned, sometimes created from intuition.

Cees Koeman: 'I was able to create slopes, create runs,

cuts in the mountain and all this, building the catwalk and building Little Beauty. I named several slopes and trails.

'It was wonderful and of course was damn hard work because everything was done with axes and saws. It was a very exciting period but we did a lot of hard work.'

The fun had an occasionally anxious edge – 'I built the catwalk from the Merritts area, Merritts Creek back to the main slopes.

'I thought it was a great job, then the snow came and the boss (Dick Dusseldorp who was a beginner skier) came from Sydney and he fell on his face several times and he said it was too steep.

'He said, "You have to make a flatter one, people want to walk". So I made a flat one the following summer and I made the Bunny Walk for him and he was happy with that.'

There were many other original trail workers – often volunteers from the village and resort workers who simply sought new skiing adventures.

Thredbo ski patroller Tommy Tomasi said he used to cut trails with his patrolling colleague Danny Collman in their own time "because you loved to see the result," (see chapter three for more on Tomasi, Collman and the patrol).

THREDBO DAWN: *With the trails groomed, the mountain is ready to run. After extensive clearing in the early days, reforestation is being used to redefine the trail network and improve snow drifting and shelter from the wind and the sun*

FROM THE AIR: *The inset shot was taken from Thyne Reid's De Havilland Drover aircraft in 1957. The single lift line belongs to the Crackenback rope tow and is the course still followed by the Kosciuszko Express chairlift. The main shot was taken in winter 2005, with a full cover over Thredbo's trails and a full cover on the Snowy Mountains, all the way to Mt Kosciuszko towards the top centre of the photograph.*

Grooming

There are some technical ambiguities when it comes to slope maintenance. Slope grooming is the summer activity which can involve removing rocks, clearing trees and undergrowth and even resowing the slope or trail, to be regularly mown to ensure good skiing and boarding on minimal snow cover.

Snow grooming is the winter activity, using oversnow machinery with blades at the front to move snow around and tillers or packers at the rear to pack and prepare it and give that smooth corduroy finish.

Thredbo's winter grooming started with a Tucker Sno-Cat in the 1960s – a machine used in the United States for grooming but one which had actually been built for oversnow transport in the Antarctic.

Cees Koeman has some romantic recollections: 'It was a beautiful machine … people would laugh at it today, but it could go almost anywhere.'

It didn't have a roller behind it, so Koeman made one from steel and aluminium.

'I tried it out in the middle of the day on the middle slopes where it was easier to manoeuvre and I looked out the rear window and someone was skiing right behind it. From that day onwards, we've had to pack the snow. It's been expected and boy, did that change skiing.' Recognising the market for the machinery, manufacturers started to build them with much wider tracks, meaning there was less pressure per square centimetre on the snow, which was a problem with the earlier machines.

Names such as Ratrac, Thiokol, Bombardier, Tucker and LMC have made their mark in oversnow and grooming machinery, but the German-built Kassbohrer PistenBully has dominated. By 1974, when Werner Siegenthaler arrived, Thredbo had two small Kassbohrer machines. Only one had a blade at the front and in those days they were much more into packing the snow.

'They were really difficult to handle – these machines were used for T-bar tracks, beginners' areas and so on. On a slope like Crackenback, there was very little done – there were moguls everywhere.'

FIRST TRACKS: *The early grooming fleet included twin-track Thiokol and four-track Tucker Sno-Cat machines. Even though they had very basic grooming attachments, their work was immediately appreciated. The machines were occasionally also used to tow skiers beyond Thredbo's summit for some runs among the Ramsheads, a practice since discontinued.*

Then Kassbohrer developed its second generation of groomers, with a solid shield at the front that could be used to cut moguls and move snow.

'Then came the rotary groomers (they had a rotating tiller at the rear) from about 1984 onwards and that's when we really started to get into big-time grooming; we had the technology to produce the slope we wanted.'

The progression was to more powerful machines and then the winch cat – a grooming machine fitted with an arm on

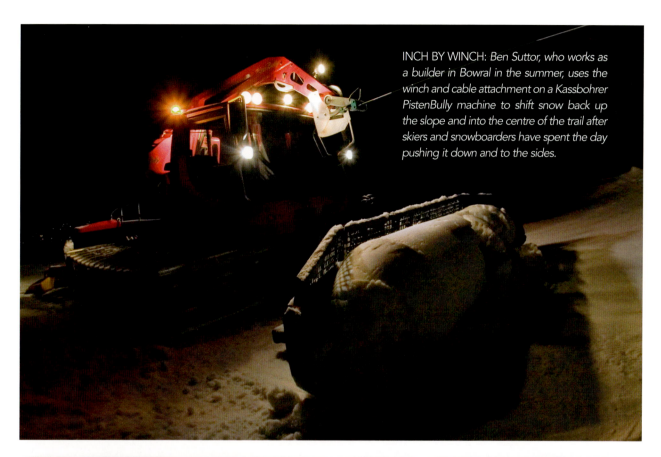

INCH BY WINCH: *Ben Suttor, who works as a builder in Bowral in the summer, uses the winch and cable attachment on a Kassbohrer PistenBully machine to shift snow back up the slope and into the centre of the trail after skiers and snowboarders have spent the day pushing it down and to the sides.*

its rear with a winch and cable; the cable is attached to an anchor point and the grooming machine operates beneath it, giving the groomers unprecedented access and flexibility on steeper slopes.

'We can now groom just about any slope on this hill – the steeps like Little Beauty, Wood Run and Funnelweb and the Supertrail,' Werner Siegenthaler said.

Grooming is an art, an exceptional skill in the hands of a resort's operational staff. Following a fall of natural snow, packing it with a groomer does two things. It compacts it and squashes the oxygen out of it, making it more durable and by creating a smoother, more even surface, it is easier for most skiers and boarders to use.

During the day, 'skiers and boarders tend to push the

snow down the slope and to the sides,' Peter Tomasi said. 'We try and pull it back up the hill and back to the centre – this is where the winch cats really come into their own.

'Because we have to work in such marginal conditions, Australian groomers are very much in demand in overseas resorts,' he said.

Kim Clifford agrees: 'Australian ski resorts probably do more with their snow than any resorts in the world, simply because we don't have much of it.

'We have to manage it, shift it and look after it. It's a very precious commodity and we have some of the world's best grooming drivers doing that.'

SURFACE TENSION: With the winch still in use, the grooming machine puts the finishing touch on the Crackenback Supertrail (above). The next morning, skier Peter Ilinsky (left), uses 2006-style skis and technique to carve his way over the corduroy surface left by the grooming machine.

Snowmaking

Snowmaking was the obvious solution to Thredbo's inability to provide reliable top-to-bottom skiing, but it took a long time for the technology to make the grade.

Albert van der Lee travelled to the United States and Canada in 1969 and 1972 specifically to look at new developments such as snowmaking.

He recalled: 'I went over to the warmest places in the east and the west where they were making snow. They were making it, but I also found that they were not as warm as Thredbo – they were much colder, especially at night.'

Nevertheless, they persevered and kept experimenting at Thredbo. 'We bought a gun and made a bit of snow here and there but it didn't really work commercially.

'I didn't get cold feet on snowmaking, but there was nowhere that it was being successfully made at the temperatures we had.

'I never would have been able to get the funds from Lend Lease to do it because there was no feasibility study to show that it would work.'

As the 1980s moved on, the technology improved. One winter in the mid-1980s, Wayne Kirkpatrick was anticipating a visit from the Lend Lease board.

'We didn't have approval (from Lend Lease) but what we did was get a water pump and a couple of snow guns and pumped the water straight out of the river next to Valley Terminal, pumped it through the snow guns and built this bloody great mound of snow.

'I knew the Lend Lease board was coming down, so we were able to say to them – "there you go, we can make snow".'

Snowmaking became part of the overall master plan that was implemented when Lend Lease sold Kosciuszko Thredbo to Amalgamated Holdings.

At the time, there were two types of snowmaking system: air/water which relied on a mixture of water and cooled, compressed air; and airless which pumped water through the larger fan guns.

In the 1980s, the air/water system was the most productive in areas with marginal temperatures and humidity. Thredbo selected it and has stuck with it, but the operation has grown substantially.

'In the first stage of snowmaking,' mountain manager Werner Siegenthaler said, 'we only had two compressors for 6000 CFM (cubic feet per minute) of air. With that, we found we could only operate about 40 guns and we had all this water that we couldn't use.

'That was a good learning curve for us – we realised that if we were going to go big time and cover the Gunbarrel and High Noon development with snowmaking, we needed more capacity.'

So they got rid of those two compressors and bought four new ones – 7500 CFM each, giving capacity for 30,000 cubic feet of air a minute and four pumps that could deliver about 7800 litres per minute of water.

The next phase of snowmaking is automation, which gives far greater productivity and use of resources.

Up until winter 2006, the system was manual, with an operator turning on the gun and adjusting it manually.

'To turn on 110 guns takes over three hours, and in that time, the temperature might have dropped or even gone up – it all takes too long to take advantage of the good conditions,' Siegenthaler said.

'With automation, we can turn on 110 guns in 15 minutes. Each group of three guns has a weather station attached and that gives information to the computer in the pumphouse which works out the right mix of air and water and sends the information back to that particular hydrant and the valve in there adjusts automatically.'

PROVING GROUND: *An early attempt at snowmaking near Valley Terminal proves the capability of the technology.*

There is a subtle difference between natural and machine-made snow. This also gives resort operators an edge.

The natural, fall-from-the-sky type of snow crystal is created when a water molecule forms around a microscopic dust particle, other water molecules then join in and the snowflake grows, from the inside outwards.

In machine made snow, the crystal is 'an aerated particle of water where the crystalisation works in reverse,' Thredbo's slopes manager, Peter Tomasi said.

'It freezes in towards the centre and that means there's always some moisture left in it.'

This means the snowmakers can create a base or cover where 'the water drains off or leeches out and that gives a much more solid, durable base. We can also make the top-up snow slightly drier for a better effect when grooming,' Tomasi said.

It's what the business types call a killer-application. Quite simply, snowmaking transformed Thredbo.

Before it was introduced there were around 18-20 days of top-to-bottom skiing, the rest of the time, people would download on the chairlifts.

Now, virtually every day of winter operation, skiers and boarders can make it to the bottom of the Crackenback Supertrail or High Noon.

FINE TUNING: *With the system automated in 2006, Thredbo could have 110 snow guns operational in 15 minutes, an operation that previously took over three hours. Snowmaking has given the resort the reliability it needed for terrain coverage and top-to-bottom skiing.*

Two skis become one

Compared with current ski technology, the skis available in Thredbo's first three decades were still of an era when the skier was battling the mountain.

Skis had very little sidecut and were used long to enhance stability and their running quality – a skier on 170cm skis today could have been on 210cm skis in the 1970s.

Great skiers were typically gifted athletes or very well taught; achieving expert level took a long time on snow. There were various attempts to change the technology. Brands such as Hart and Graves from the United States and Lacroix from France introduced shorter skis during the 1970s, but they didn't catch on.

Another US brand, Hexcel, introduced the swallow tail on skis and that innovation found some fans. The swallow tail also had devotees among surfers in the 1970s and they too sought to make their mark on the mountain, but with something more like their surfboard than the 'boards' the skiers were using.

Geoff Sawyer, who grew up in Sydney surfing with the Long Reef Boardriders, first encountered snowboarding

SKI STYLE: *Skiing technique is as much about following the teachings of the time as it is about exploiting equipment to its fullest. Tommy Tomasi (below) shows perfect, stylish form in 1960 while Stuart Diver (right), explodes in the style of a new century in 2000.*

as a traveller when he spent the season working in the US at Aspen Highlands in 1983-84.

'The only snowboards I came across that year were these wooden Burton laminated boards – no high-back bindings, no steel edges, no P-tex or anything, just a wooden veneer thing and you used to iron wax on to them.

'I came back the following season (1984-85) and worked at Highlands again, in the ski shop at the bottom of the mountain.

'I did the ski tuning at night – I'd get that done and then a couple of guys and I – Chris Karol and another guy

ON BOARD: *Snowboarding pioneer Geoff Sawyer (below) rides his 1986 Burton swallow tail board on Thredbo's Cannonball run. Twenty years later, a competitor takes a hit on course on High Noon. The essential style difference is in the hands – Sawyer was expressing himself like a freestyle skier, the other boarder is grabbing his board like a skateboarder. In the photograph overleaf, Trent Glaser carves a powder turn on a winter morning beyond The Basin.*

called Jeff Grell (Grell invented the high-back snowboard binding) would go out riding.'

Snowboarding was banned at the time at Aspen Highlands, so they would use a snowmobile, typically on a moonlit night, to access the slopes and try out the snowboards.

After that winter (1984-85), Sawyer returned to Australia with three snowboards under his arm and the rights to import Burton boards. He moved to Jindabyne for the winter and started riding his board at Perisher Valley.

'After the first or second day of riding at Perisher, I stupidly went into the office – I wanted to import the boards but I had to be sure you could use them – so I introduced myself and explained what I was doing and said "do you mind if I do it?"

'And they said, "Well, yeah, we do mind".

'They made me go outside and do a demo and they said, "No, you're too dangerous."

Sawyer didn't repeat the mistake. He went to Thredbo and bought a season's pass for winter 1985: 'I didn't ask, I just went out riding.'

He didn't draw a lot of attention to himself – the board wouldn't handle moguls or hard-packed terrain so he was typically riding off-piste in areas such as the Golf Course or on more remote runs such as Cannonball.

He recalled seeing monoskiers at Thredbo at the time – David Lee was one – but he didn't recall seeing any other snowboarders in that 1985 season.

'That same year I met up with Paul Bow and Don McInnes who were both working with the Thredbo Ski School and had just written the first Australian ski teaching methodology.'

At this time he started getting involved with the ski school – Sawyer realised that to get snowboards selling, there had to be formal acceptance and a teaching method. At Thredbo, he started to achieve both.

By the next winter, 1986, the groundswell had started and by the late 1980s snowboarding was becoming accepted throughout the skiing world – Thredbo was a host on a national competition circuit and its first halfpipe was built in the Basin area.

In the technology of the equipment, Sawyer said what really set the snowboarding world on fire was the combination of deeper sidecuts, softer flex and shorter boards. It also put a fire under ski manufacturers.

Realising their market of younger skiers was vanishing into snowboarding, they responded with shorter skis that

had deeper sidecuts and were much easier to turn and teach on; much more versatile in their application.

For mountain manager Werner Siegenthaler, this represented a huge change on the mountain: 'In the old days, we used to groom the slope and by 10am you wouldn't know where the groomer had been.

'Before the shaped ski came in, virtually all skiers were tail sliding on the down side of a mogul and you created the moguls by skiing in the valley of the mogul.

'With the carve skis that has all changed – you give it pressure and it just wants to go around; that's a sensational, exhilarating feeling.'

Thredbo 3 people

What's an alpine resort without romance? Michelle and Heinz Reichinger's lives in Thredbo are a window into the life of the village.

In 1971, a young Michelle Slutzkin, not long out of school and recently returned from a trip to Europe, made her way down to Thredbo with a family friend, Walter Dusseldorp, one of Dick Dusseldorp's children. Michelle put it like this:

'I had been here once before, in 1964 – the year of the big snow. I thought it was very charming and because that was such a great snow season, I thought it was a very romantic European village, very enchanting.

'My father, Alexander Slutzkin, was a businessman, a publican with hotels in Sydney – the Cross and Enfield – and different parts of New South Wales. With a few partners who were chemists at the time, they took the leases on the grocery store and chemist and the snack bar at Thredbo. That was in the upper concourse, probably just prior to 1964.

'I came here in 1971 and I met Heinz (Reichinger) who was a ski instructor – he was Ann Dusseldorp's private ski instructor but I don't think I knew that at the time.

'When they left, I said, "I've got nothing to go back to in Sydney, I think I'll stay on and finish the season here and I'll look for a job."

'So I got a position with Rudi Schatzle, working at the Eagles Nest at the top of Crackenback.

'I settled in as a worker-cum-holiday maker and I learnt to ski and that winter I met Heinz, my husband.

'I wasn't planning to meet the man of my dreams, my future husband but … as it happened, by the end of that winter, we had decided to go over to Sun Valley [USA] together, where he was instructing in the alternate season.

'Whilst we were over there, we got married in Sun Valley, in January of 1972. How romantic! It was a beautiful resort – it is like our other home in many ways.

'I obtained my residency while I was there because Heinz

had a residency as a working Austrian, with his skills.

'So I thought, "Oh well, this will be our life, we'll live in America and decide on our future."

'Before we could really make any future plans, my father sent us a letter or a telegram and said that if we came back to Australia we could take over the business in Thredbo and run that.

'I think he knew that was the only way he would get us back! The mountain came back to get us – I think he knew that Heinz wasn't going to be able to live in a place that didn't remind him of his homeland.

'We thought about it briefly and decided that would be a great way to establish ourselves in business and came back for that season, for the 1972 winter.'

Heinz Reichinger was born in Innsbruck and grew up skiing some of the local areas such as Axamer Lizum and first came to Australia to work as a ski instructor in 1964 (see the snow sports section in this chapter).

He remembered those early days in this way: 'The close-knit friendships in the ski school and the adventure of coming out here was enough for us to get excited. We really had a marvellous time.

'And of course, I met Michelle in 1971 and that changed everything for me. She walked into the village and had a holiday here and she decided to stay.

'She worked up at Eagles Nest at the top of the mountain for Rudi Schatzle who had most of the places here on the mountain.

'We met and fell in love and I took her over to Sun Valley for a year and then we came back in 1972 and took over the business here in Thredbo.

'It was actually a general store, had everything – the souvenirs, the delicatessen, the snack bar, the groceries, the hardware. I then stopped instructing.

'We had our families here, the kids were born here in Thredbo and we built some apartments.'

In their second year as Thredbo business people, the shop next door became vacant – it had been a hairdressing salon – so Michelle and Heinz expanded their groceries business and developed a better chemist and souvenir shop.

'When Dougie Edwards set up a supermarket down the road, we realised it would be difficult for us to compete against that, so we went heavily into the delicatessen, brought in a lot

LEAP OF FAITH: *With his fellow patrollers surrounding him, Tommy Tomasi jumps the camera on Crackenback. The photographer used a fisheye lens and triggered the shot by remote control; the photograph first appeared in the Melbourne* Sun *newspaper in 1971.*

73

PUSHING THEIR LUCK: *Like the rest of Australia's high country, Thredbo village had a deep cover in 1964; getting around wasn't easy.*

of imported foods, flew in a lot of fresh small goods from Sydney and that ran quite successfully,' Michelle said.

Around 1981 they decided they'd move into clothing and skiwear; by 1982, 'my shop was running as Michelle's and then Heinz converted the snack bar, which we were also running at the time, from Heinz's Hots to Heinz's Ski Tech which became a men's wear and equipment store.'

They developed a routine of going to Europe, visiting Heinz's family and visiting clothing and skiwear factories to 'bring back our own exclusive labels. We had a lot of fun.'

When their sons Luke and Marcus left school, they too became involved with the business.

'We opened a snowboard shop down at Valley Terminal called Shredbo. At that time Heinz was getting a little weary of running his store and our boys went in there and relocated the snowboard shop from Valley Terminal to the concourse and that became known as the Good Board Store.

'They saw it as a niche, an opportunity. They were both ski racers, but they converted.

'They ran it for some years before they finally decided they had to move on and find a life outside the village where they were born.'

Together with Frank Prihoda and Helmut Steinoecker, an instructor who came to Thredbo in the 1960s, Heinz and Michelle built the Frankheinzstein's apartments off Bobuck Lane. Frank Prihoda is Sasha Nekvapil's brother. He fled Czechoslovakia with his brother-in-law Karel Nekvapil in January 1949 and came to Australia early in 1950 to work in the occupation in which he'd been trained – the manufacture of artificial flowers.

Frank worked away in Melbourne but maintained a connection with the snow and skied for Australia in slalom and giant slalom at the 1956 Cortina Olympics.

He would visit Sasha and Karel in Thredbo and 'wanted to come to Thredbo, to have some business, but there was nothing really here until the year 1974.

'Then a shop became vacant here which was down in the lower concourse in the hotel where the Keller Bar is now.

'So I took the shot and I came in 1974. In the meantime of course, I was coming here for lots of holidays. Maybe twice a winter for a weekend but I spent Christmas holidays and Easter here, did a lot of fishing,' Prihoda said.

He first ran the shop as an arts and crafts business, later changing to the more popular souvenirs and gifts, a prosperous business that he ran until 2001.

'When I turned 80, I said, "That's enough".'

The lifestyle in Thredbo drew Frank Prihoda and has never really lost its appeal: 'Thredbo's the best place in Australia to live. We have good weather, we have lovely summers, we get it warm and hot at times but it nearly always cools down at night and we have enough water … these days that's a great blessing.'

The appeal has also endured for Heinz Reichinger. 'Apart from the hard yakka in the main season, we've got a lifestyle in the summer when the business is slower and you can go away for walks and go away for a holiday.

'You're out in the open; you can do a lot of things. At the drop of a hat you can just ring someone and before you know it you've got a little dinner party … that sort of thing you couldn't do in the city.'

Michelle recalled raising a family in a place like Thredbo as 'pretty special. Having them in this little fishbowl down here. There were a lot of other young families as well; it was a pretty special time down here in the 1970s and 1980s.

'It was very much a family-run resort still and a lot of people who were here were about our age, they were running their own businesses and lodges and having lots of bubbers.

'It was a very constructive, busy time. The boys were lucky that they had a lot of peers here that they grew up with and started and went through school with, some of them right to the end of high school.

'The village was really their back yard; I think they thought they owned the mountain really. They were very comfortable with the great outdoors, with nature and they weren't frightened of the dark. They had their own little swimming holes, sacred meeting places.'

Commercial lodges

People like to belong, no more so than in an alpine resort, and they like to be made to feel as though they belong. Recognition is the difference between a stranger and a guest.

In the European tradition, the ski lodge hosts were as important as identities as the ski instructors. It gave the village depth and continuity if guests could by greeted and acknowledged by their hosts year after year.

Suzanne and Kornel Deseo opened the first commercial lodge, Candlelight, in 1958 and were said by Dick Dusseldorp to excel at the art.

They were soon followed by Sasha and Karel Nekvapil who built the first stage of their lodge, Sasha's, in 1959.

'We started building in January 1959 and opened in June 1959 … we only had £1600 and we had to borrow the rest of the money, it was very expensive and worrying,' Sasha Nekvapil said.

Their architect Otto Ernegg designed the lodge so that half of it was completed and operational for the 1959 winter and the other half was built three years later, when they had some more money.

'In the first half, we had 15 guests and when we built the second half, we had about 34 guests.'

For the guest in a commercial lodge, the operation should always appear to be running smoothly, but appearances can be deceiving. At Sasha's, things weren't always straightforward in the kitchen.

'Sometimes they (the chefs) were not very satisfactory, they would have to go and then my husband (Karel) would have to start cooking.

'Some were just very poor cooks, one was a drunkard, one was always vanishing to go to the races … one put a pound of salt into everything, we couldn't have that.'

But they also had some success with their chefs – 'One of them was here for only one season, he became the most celebrated chef in Sydney – Tony Bilson.'

It can be a demanding occupation. Karel and Sasha would open all year round, so they were never able to take a holi-day together. They ran the lodge for 12 years and when they sold it, it became the Black Bear Inn.

Life became much easier running the apartments, Sasha said, although she had a shop – Sasha's Sportswear – as part of that enterprise.

The Clifford family built Winterhaus in 1961 and ran it until 1973; the winter season was always busy, but so were Christmas and Easter.

Kim Clifford said: 'We actually lived here in winter time, for all of primary school and did correspondence in winter and we used to go back to our family home in Sydney, but we were always here for all of the school holidays.

'Winterhaus would open at Christmas and Easter; it'd be busy around Christmas. People from central Europe – a lot of them were relatively new refugees – they'd do what they did in Europe and go to the mountains. They were the main source of summer business in those early days.'

HOLDING THE FLAME: *Suzanne and Kornel Deseo photographed in 1958. They built Candlelight, Thredbo's first commercial lodge, and ran it for 20 years.*

Ski clubs

Thredbo's quirky nature, its sense of humour, is no recent occurrence. Consider this report from the Crackenback Ski Club, in the 1957 *Australian Ski Year Book*.

'The club was officially formed on December 17, 1956 and now has over 90 members. At an unofficial inaugural meeting last August, a majority of those present were persuaded by Jimmy Walker to vote in favour of calling the club the Dead Horse Ski Club.'

'However, an interim committee appointed at that meeting contained five lawyers who proved to their own entire satisfaction that Walker had put up both hands when Dead Horse won by one vote. A protest by the Crackenback faction was therefore upheld.'

'The Dead Horsemen have appealed and a referendum will be held at the next annual general meeting to decide finally what we will call ourselves. Apparently the Dead Horsemen do not yet realise that the lawyers have so drafted the constitution that any change of name must be proved by one hundred per cent of the members.'

'Between battles on the name question, the committee has found time to let a contract for the construction of a ten-bunk hut at Friday Flat for a contract price of £5600. The hut site has an excellent view of the Thredbo River and Ramshead Range and is only fifty yards from the proposed bottom station of the Crackenback Peak Chair Lift.'

The following year, the club reported (*ASYB* 1958) that, with the erection of its hut early in July, 1957, it was the 'proud possessor of the first building in what is now becoming a thriving alpine village at Friday Flat on the Thredbo.'

During the 1957 NSW State Championships, for which the club was appointed host, Snowy Mountains Authority (SMA) commissioner Sir William Hudson formally opened the club hut.

'There are many difficulties inherent in being the first organisation to become established in a new area. But there are also certain material advantages: revenue from the accommodation at the Hut far exceeded our expectations and in the result we are not quite so destitute as we had resigned ourselves to being.

'Indeed, the combination of a modest profit and judicious assistance from a benign bank manager has enabled us to go ahead with our programme of improvements rather faster than we had anticipated.' (*ASYB*, 1958)

With one of the syndicate's founding directors, Geoffrey Hughes and his family to drive it, Crackenback had Thredbo's first ski club lodge, but the Thredbo Alpine Club (TAC) was hot on its heels with the enthusiasm that typically drives successful ski clubs.

The original catchment for TAC members was Sydney University – its Sports Union had a club lodge at Guthega and the quality, or more particularly, the lack of it, was one of the main motivating factors for the move to Thredbo.

In a 2004 TAC newsletter, the late James Cunningham, a founding TAC member, recalled his first visit to Thredbo in 1957 with Jim Bibby.

'There was a fearsome rope tow running at high speed and its only run down through the trees was steep, icy and designed for champions.

'There was one prefabricated Norwegian building which was the manager's flat and hotel accommodation on the first floor and bar with ski room below … the only other building was Crackenback Ski Club.'

Other Sydney University students visited Thredbo during that first year and liked what they saw; among them were Ben Salmon and David Ross, who met with Cunningham and Bibby in October 1957 to talk about forming a club and building a lodge at Thredbo.

They wanted a manageable enterprise so decided to put a ceiling of 60 members on the club and eight beds on the lodge.

What came next was a reflection of the underlying demand for snow sports and accommodation in the mountains.

'We decided to test the water,' Cunningham wrote, 'The principle sources for potential members were the SU (Sydney University) Ski Club, the law and architectural faculties and the colleges.'

CRACKENBACK: *Thredbo's first club, under construction in April 1957 (below left) and open for accommodation in August 1957 (above), when it was the host club for the NSW State Championships.*

Within a few weeks, they had more than 300 applicants, so they decided to enlarge the lodge to 16 beds and the memberships to 150.

The initial obligation for members was to pay a £50 joining fee and to give at least a week's labour to the building of the lodge in Thredbo.

They were resourceful and innovative. 'The walls under the floor beneath the fireplace and the rock wall are thick and substantial. We did not want to waste stone on them so they consist of a 100mm concrete block wall on either side and a rubble filling.'

That filling is of beer, wine, scotch and gin bottles – 'It is an engineering fact that unbroken bottles form a very strong filling and their use saved stone or rubble.

'The group at Thredbo for Easter [1958] went around all the clubs in the village at the end of the holidays, like garbage men, and collected bottles left over from the parties.

'This was one morning's work which yielded about 100 dozen bottles which are concreted into these walls.'

Steven Szeloczky, a member of the Hungarian rowing eight who all defected following the 1956 Melbourne Olympics, was working in the village at the time.

He commented to Cunningham that in Hungary they had a tradition of putting a gold sovereign under the fireplace as an omen for the future of the house.

'He joked that it was easy to predict the future of TAC.' Club life was congenial and collegiate – a shared passion for the mountains, for the sport and for the good times.

An early club member, Susan Sypkens (nee Oddie), had her 21st birthday at the club, in August 1958, celebrating with 'cake and champagne sent from Cooma … the living room was packed to overflowing with everyone singing rude songs.' Her August 1959 birthday was at Kareela, at the top of the chairlift. 'As penniless students, Mary Macoun and I got jobs as casual chairlift attendants – for each half day's work we received two day's free chairlift rides,' Sypkens wrote in a March 2005 TAC newsletter.

Kareela and Roslyn were two projects with close links to one of the most active clubs of the era, the Ski Tourers' Association which later became known as the Australian Alpine Club.

Writing in the 1959 *Australian Ski Year Book*, STA president Charles Anton described the first winter of operations.

'Roslyn Lodge was completed in June 1958 and Foundation Memberships in the project total 300.

'All facilities worked well and John Turner excelled in managing the lodge. From July onwards, the 22-bed hut was usually filled to capacity and on some weekends, Roslyn has accommodated up to 25 visitors.

'Early in the new year, a simple bronze plaque, designed by Verna (Venn) Wesche in memory of his daughter Roslyn was placed in the living room.

'A number of improvements and innovations are planned for

this summer, but essentially the lodge, which cost us more than £10,000, is finished.'

Roslyn relocated to a new building on its current site on Bobuck Lane in 1976; the original Roslyn Lodge became High Noon and was rebuilt in 1995.

Following the completion of the first stage of the Crackenback chairlift in 1958, Charles Anton played his dual roles at Thredbo – the driver of the Ski Tourers' Association and a member of the Kosciuszko Chairlift and Thredbo Hotel Syndicate – with typical energy.

Anton wrote that, after the construction of the chairlift, it seemed logical to use it to transport materials for a lodge '… which (it is hoped) will form the nucleus of the future Upper Thredbo Village.'

That lodge was Kareela, in its original form designed by Austrian architect, Otto Ernegg, who also designed Sasha's Lodge. Its main feature was a V-shaped front with large windows to overlook the Thredbo Valley.

The trade-off for Kareela's members to use the chairlift in the construction of the lodge was to run a public restaurant for the resort in its first season.

That facility was closed after 1959 'as it interferes with the convenience and privacy of resident members.'

However, Anton wrote with satisfaction that an important new development was the installation of a gas-operated floodlight 'at the top chairlift station and consequent permission of the Department of Labour and Industry to operate the lift at night. 'This caters well for the future top village and will enable Kareela residents to take part in the nightlife at Thredbo Alpine Village if they wish to do so.

'Kareela is the ideal spot for those who want to live in the snow and at the same time enjoy all the facilities of the new Thredbo area, Australia's fastest-growing alpine resort.' (ASYB 1959)

A village at altitude was mooted for both the Kareela and Merritts areas but it has never eventuated.

Kosciuszko Thredbo bought Kareela in 1962 and it has operated as a day lodge or restaurant ever since.

It had a vibrant few seasons as a club lodge though, with more than 100 people attending a roof-raising ceremony in May 1959.

Among the guests were 'SMA commissioner Sir William Hudson, members of Federal and State Parliaments, executives of the Kosciuszko State Park Trust and representatives of Ski Clubs … Sir Wilfred Kent-Hughes, Federal MP and former Minister for the Interior – an inveterate skier – and Lady Kent-Hughes performed the ceremony.'

Anton and his fellow syndicate members saw the value of including dignitaries in the resort's activities.

Late in August 1959, Kareela was officially opened by the Federal Treasurer (later Prime Minister), Harold Holt.

An anonymous report on Thredbo in the 1958 *Australian Ski Year Book*, anticipated 10 or 12 ski club huts and guest houses, completed for the winter of 1958.

They included 'Ski Club of Australia, Ramshead Ski Club, Youth Hostels Association, Ski Tourers' Association (Roslyn), Thredbo Alpine Club, the Candlelight Lodge (being built by Kornel and Suzanne Deseo) together with a number of smaller huts being built by new clubs – Rainbow, Sequoia and Neewalla and several, as yet unnamed, huts.'

Geebung was another of the early ski clubs, built by a Berridale builder Kurt Springer and named after Banjo Paterson's poem, *The Geebung Polo Club*.

According to its own published history, the first lodge was completed and occupied in 1959 and was 'built simply as a small mountain retreat for 25 members. This was later increased to 50 members.

'The lodge consisted of four small rooms with a three-quarter bunk on the bottom and a single bunk on top, and the rooms each measured six feet by ten feet. There were four bunkrooms and two shower rooms.

'There was also a loft, which was a very popular spot. The loft was entered through a trapdoor, and would never have passed any fire or building regulations today as the chimney went up through it. This room was naturally very warm, and many interesting and amusing events took place up there.

'The sundeck, which is there today, is the original, which was kept when the new lodge was built.

'The living area is almost the same but bigger. In the original lodge everything was on the same level and the only entrance was the front door. There was a ladder attached to the loft window on the Candlelight side to be used as a fire escape but luckily it was never required.' (Geebung internet site, 2006)

Creating clubs hasn't always been plain sailing. Redbank Lodge, the club building of the Alpine Association of Australia, is said to have been established as a result of the disenchantment of one of the members of the Happy Wanderers club next door.

He wandered away from that group and, in the early 1960s, established the Alpine Association.

The conflict doesn't seem to have done either entity any enduring damage – Redbank is well used in winter by a club with around 75 members from Sydney and beyond, while the Happy Wanderers and its 150-odd members are currently working on a redevelopment of their lodge.

The proliferation of apartments and private chalets or lodges in Thredbo's new estates, such as Crackenback Ridge and Woodridge has strengthened the view that clubs are on the wane.

If they're simply looked at in the mix of new property development, the view has some credibility, but that misses the point that many of Thredbo's clubs, and in particular many of its older clubs, have very healthy and active memberships; people who retain their enthusiasm for the resort in summer and winter.

KAREELA: *Roof-raising day at Kareela Hutte in 1959 (left), Thredbo's highest accommodation. Despite Charles Anton's ambitions, the high-altitude village never eventuated at Thredbo and Kareela reverted to a day lodge in 1962.*
REDBANK: *Brian Chater (below left) Gerry Hampson and Bob Snedden working below the original Redbank building in 1962.*

Ski patrol

When the first skiers rode the Crackenback chairlift in the 1958 winter, the Thredbo Ski Patrol was on duty, even if it comprised just two people – Tommy Tomasi and Danny Collman.

Tommy Tomasi was raised among the mountains of Italy where he had skied competitively up until the Second World War.

He served as a partisan in a divided Italy, fighting the Fascists and Germans until caught, imprisoned and tortured by the German Gestapo in 1944.

With Europe falling to the Allies, one night his prison guards simply disappeared. Tomasi, weighing just 32kg after his ordeal, escaped, to eventually be found by passing Americans and nursed back to health.

With his partisan background working against him in postwar Italy, he decided to emigrate.

Tomasi landed in Fremantle and worked in the West as a miner for a time, but once he heard there was snow in Australia, he made for Cooma, working for the Snowy Hydro Scheme and, in winter 1953, at the Kosciuszko Chalet at Charlotte Pass.

He returned to the SMA in 1955 and joined the hydrology branch where he worked alongside Collman, recording snow depths, stream flows and weather.

Danny Collman, from Jindabyne, was an excellent skier; Geoffrey Hughes said he was unlucky to miss the Olympics; a Victorian got his spot 'because they had to balance out NSW and Victoria … skiing politics is just like real politics.'

RESCUE: *The uniforms have changed a little and the Akja rescue sleds have a slightly different build, but the patrolling basics are the same. Tommy Tomasi (at front) and John Rumble on the Crackenback slopes in 1961.*

GOLD MEDAL COMPANY: *Patroller Tommy Tomasi outside Valley Terminal in 1962 with one of the greatest skiers of the era, Norway's Stein Eriksen, who won gold in the giant slalom and silver in the slalom at the 1952 Oslo Winter Olympics. Eriksen was the first skier from outside the European Alps to win an alpine Olympic medal. He was in Thredbo to make a movie with John Jay called* Winter Magic Around the World.

Once Thredbo's Syndicate had the resort under way, Tomasi and Collman looked at the prospects for a patrol – it was something Tomasi had discussed with Charles Anton a few years previously at the Kosciuszko Chalet.

'Being a skier from a long way back and having participated in many rescues in Italy, the idea of a ski patrol was something that attracted me because an accident could happen to me,' Tomasi said.

'In 1957, Danny Collman and I … decided to start a patrol. In the hydrology department, it was compulsory to hold a first aid certificate in case something happened to us on the mountain and we had to look after ourselves.'

The opening weekend in 1958 was the patrol's first day of service and while there was only one lift operating, Tomasi and Collman needed some back-up to cover the fledgling ski field – as volunteers, they couldn't do it alone for the entire season.

'It was very difficult then to get good skiers that were prepared to devote their time to patrolling,' Tomasi said.

Nevertheless, they managed to recruit some other workers from the SMA's hydrology branch as well as skiers from Jindabyne and Cooma.

'By the beginning of July 1958, we had about a dozen patrollers, that was sufficient because we didn't have to spread the patrol over a big area.'

In that first season, Tomasi recalled there were few cut trails for skiers '… you could come down in many ways, however the general public just followed the main trail under the chairlift.'

Effective communications are essential for ski patrolling; in its infancy, some resorts would resort to semaphore, using flags to alert patrollers to an accident, but Tomasi and Collman were ahead of the game with technology.

They installed a telephone cable along the Crackenback lift line in summer 1957-58 and buried it before winter. That meant in the event of an accident, a skier could contact the lift operator who in turn would alert the patrol – still a common means of notifying the patrol.

Tomasi, Collman and their fellow patrollers started using radios in the 1960s; they are now widespread and indispensable.

Recognising the importance of the patrol, the syndicate first provided it with a room above the chairlift bottom station; it had three beds but they shook like an old car on a corrugated road when the chairlift started up.

When Valley Terminal was built in the 1960s, the patrol's accommodation expanded to a 25-bed dormitory and then in the early 1990s, when Woodridge Estate was first being developed, Kosciuszko Thredbo donated two blocks of land at Woodridge to the patrol. One block was for Sundowner Lodge, the new accommodation base for volunteer patrollers, the other was for the patrol to sell or develop – to raise funds to cover the cost of the building.

The volunteer component of a body like a ski patrol brings together an extraordinary range of skills – architects, doctors, lawyers and farmers and a range of trades.

'There was a core half a dozen patrollers,' Thredbo's current ski patrol manager David Kuhn said, 'people who really put some effort in, there were some really good carpenters on the patrol who did a lot. At one stage they had 16 apprentices working there for free to get some experience.'

SACRED HEIGHTS: *The blessing of the snow in the 1960s. John Rumble (left), Tommy Tomasi, George Weiss, George Freuden, Ludwig Rabina, John Barclay, Adrian Studley and in front, Father George Collins (left) and the Reverend R Bush.*

While Thredbo's Ski Patrol is by definition one organisation, the volunteers have their own captain and committee, with Kosciuszko Thredbo's patrol manager serving on the volunteer committee.

'We all work together on the mountain and do our training together,' David Kuhn said.

From the 12-strong volunteer group brought together by Danny Collman and Tommy Tomasi in 1958, the patrol has grown to comprise 23 paid patrollers and 70 volunteers who each commit to work for a minimum 15 days each season.

David Kuhn started as a professional patroller in 1984, when the paid patrol expanded from five to seven.

The growth in the size of the patrol, and particularly the paid patrol, was a direct response to the growth in skier numbers and, significantly, the way people skied and rode the mountain. From the late 1980s onwards, faster, more efficient lifts made the patrol more versatile and responsive, but alongside the development of supertrails, better grooming and better equipment, skiers and boarders started going faster too.

'It was conducive to speed – we made it too good and that brought on the speed patrol, we had to try and slow people down,' Kuhn said.

'Thredbo used to have a separate mountain awareness and speed patrol crew. Now we've taken that work on board in the patrol.'

Alpine resorts are a rich mix of cultures – that's obvious in the profile of Thredbo's founders, in the origins of its snow sports instructors and also in its ski patrol.

Thredbo has run exchanges with Canadian resorts such as Silver Star, Big White and Whistler, with Heavenly Valley, Squaw Valley and Big Bear in California, with Vail and Aspen in Colorado and with more obscure areas such as Okimo in Vermont, in the eastern United States.

One of its longest-running relationships has been with Val d'Isere in France, an exchange that has run since 1982.

'That exchange is huge,' David Kuhn said. 'It's a huge mountain and the lifestyle, the language and the culture are very different.

'It isn't easy but you feel enlightened when you leave, it's a big life experience that one.'

The exchange of ideas and culture enriches all the patrols involved and also gives patrollers the potential for something approaching year-round employment in the profession.

As a pioneer among Australian resorts, with arguably the first

ski patrol (Mt Buller had a rescue service but this was not for-malised into a ski patrol until the 1960s) Thredbo's ski patrol played a pioneering role in mountain safety and the forma-tion of what is now the governing body, the Australian Ski Patrol Association.

Thredbo's doctor, Steve Breathour along with patrollers David Kuhn and Tony Weaver – Kuhn's predecessor as patrol man-ager who died in 1997 in the road collapse – were major par-ticipants in the creation of the first training manual for Australian patrollers.

While the patrol is heavily supported by Kosciuszko Thredbo, they have always raised additional funds for equipment.

'In the early days, some of the people, would say, "Oh look at these bludgers, they are here only for free skiing",' Tommy Tomasi said.

'They didn't actually realise that we didn't get paid, it was all voluntary. We even had to pay for our uniform. Even now the volunteer patroller has to pay half of it, but now we also have major sponsors like Toyota.'

In his 80th year, Tommy Tomasi is still active in the patrol he

DAWN PATROL: *Thredbo ski patrol manager David Kuhn (left) and lift manager Peter Fleming get the mountain ready to ride. Safety checks are essential to open and close the slopes; first tracks can be a welcome perk for patrollers.*

founded and still in love with the sport. 'I've been skiing since four years old. I used to race back home, I was particularly good on the downhill side – mad about speed.'

That saw him on skis around 216cm or even as long as 220cm on the Golden Eagle run at Kunama in the 1950s.

He now rides a 175cm ski. 'I'm sponsored by Rossignol – they say, "Oh Tommy, you should go down to 160-165." I say, "Uh-uh. There is a limit."'

'The equipment is so far ahead that I don't think that they can improve anymore unless they put a little jet on the back.'

Snow sports schools

An expression of anticipation in the 1958 *Australian Ski Year Book*: 'Perhaps the most interesting item of news about Thredbo from a skiing viewpoint, is that the Austrian instructors, Leonard Erharter and Helmut Pfister are coming out from Zurs.

'Erharter is said to be an outstanding stylist, even in Austria, and coached our (Australian) Olympic team in 1956. Maybe the combination of big lifts, top instructors, and easy access at Thredbo will some day produce an Olympic medal winner from Australia.'

In skiing at this time, the Arlberg technique held sway and the Austrians were colonising the skiing world with it.

That technique was attributed to Hannes Schneider who was born in Stuben in Austria's Arlberg region in 1890 and went on to work in nearby St Anton, where he developed the skiing style and its progressive steps.

Like Charles Anton, Schneider was a victim of the Nazi Anschluss and in the late 1930s he moved to New Hampshire in the United States and started teaching his technique to the Americans.

Knowledge is power. At the time of Thredbo's establishment, qualified instructors were scarce in Australia. Skiers were generally self-taught or glimpsed the basics as part of a large group listening to one of the few instructors around.

Little wonder then, that the Austrian experts were hailed; they were the rock stars of the snow, celebrities in the village, performers on the mountain and keepers of the knowledge.

By the time Heinz Reichinger arrived in Thredbo in 1967, he recalled the ski school as having grown from the original two to about 35 instructors for the entire season, swelling to 50 in peak season.

Reichinger went through an unusual hiring process. He recalled arriving in Thredbo one Saturday morning and walking across the bridge to Valley Terminal with a friend.

EARLY TURNS: *Winter 1958 and Tom Hughes (at left, later Federal Attorney General and Queen's counsel) makes for the slopes with Thredbo's first instructors, Helmut Pfister and Leonard Erharter.*

SCHOOL'S IN: *In the 1960s, the ski school grew and kept growing. From left, Leonard Erharter, Walter Perwein, Sven Coomer, Walter Auer, Karl Berchtold, Helmut Steinoecker, Gernot Schermer and Sigi Wolf.*

'A mate of mine, Leonard Erharter who happened to be the chief instructor, said, "Hey boys I heard about you having trouble over at Perisher, you're going to start the class at two o'clock here",' Reichinger said.

The 'trouble at Perisher' was a fairly straightforward boy/girl type of conflict.

'One of my best mates … took a more than welcome interest in my girlfriend and I told him to buzz off and look for his own girls and that sort of soured the relationship,' Reichinger said.

The 'best mate' was Perisher's ski school director who pulled rank on Reichinger, so, after instructing at Perisher since 1964, Reichinger found himself a Thredbo instructor in 1967.

He didn't look back; he'd only been in Thredbo Village for two hours and he was working.

'In those days we really had a fantastic time, everything was very, very personal and we had a great personal contact with all the skiers who came here, in private lessons as well as in classes,' Reichinger said.

'At the end of the day, we just went to the lodges and continued there. We never had any problems to socialise in the village.

'We'd go to Bursills, to Black Bear, a lot of private lodges. We were always welcome … as soon as we walked in they'd start to scream and the grog came out … we had a marvellous time.'

Reichinger's routine was typical of the instructors at the time and is a path many still follow. They would have a return trip to Australia paid for and would work the northern season in Europe or the United States.

'I went to Kitzbuhel and skied for the Red Devils (ski school) for two or three seasons and then I went up to Obertauern and skied with some good friends up there, then I went over to Sun Valley in the States for five years and skied over there.'

The composition of ski schools throughout Australia started to change in the 1970s. As the sport boomed in participation, the demand for instructors had to be filled beyond the traditional Austrian source.

Brad Spalding, Thredbo's Snow Sports director from 1994 to 2005 started in the profession during that era.

'It was all about growth. When I started in the 70s, there was just huge growth in the ski industry, you had a lot of new skiers, it was affordable, they packaged it up so that it was really affordable so you got huge numbers of people coming to ski school.

'The growth in the 1970s and into the 1980s meant that we needed the home-grown instructor; the Austrian influence in the training of these instructors had given us a pretty strict syllabus and training program but … we really needed Australians to get into it and treat it as a career and a profession.

'That happened right across Australia and now we have Australian instructors that have settled here. They've bought houses in Jindabyne, their families are here, their kids are growing up here and they're still teaching skiing so they really have made a career of it,' Spalding said.

He started his career at Falls Creek in Victoria and visited Thredbo as a trainer and examiner for the Australian Professional Snowsports Instructors association (APSI), the profession's governing body in Australia.

'We did a lot of training and a lot of our courses in Thredbo. I just loved the skiing. I just thought it was such a great place with such great fall lines.'

The evolution of the ski school with a band of instructors running group and private lessons into a snow sports department with specialist programs and vast children's facilities has been dramatic.

In the 1970s and 1980s, according to Brad Spalding, 'Just dealing with those numbers we were sometimes on overload. 'Now we work a lot on controlling our class sizes, giving the customers a more individual experience where the instructors actually get to know the customers.'

Which sounds close to the experience and interchange that worked so well for Heinz Reichinger and his clients in the 1960s and early 1970s.

Reichinger's ski school director, Leonard Erharter, was followed by Arnold Konrad, Roland Wanner, Brad Spalding and now Adam Hosie.

'All of the other directors had done great things but I could really see from a skiing side that you could really put together great programs here,' Spalding said.

Spalding's talents go beyond skiing and ski instructing – he is also an accomplished artist and managed to bring all that together in the Thredbo Snow Sports programs.

The seeds were sown at Falls Creek, where he developed a children's program that first associated animals with skier levels.

'Thredbo was an opportunity to take the animal basis for teaching kids to the next level, so the animals actually came to life, like mascots and then we went into animal theatre and entertaining kids through the animals.

'Now we've got a professionally produced CD with kids choirs in the background … it's gone from drawing a few animals in Falls Creek to coming to Thredbo and really bringing those animals to life and they become a part of the total kids experience.

'Not only do they relate to them as a level of skiing, they believe in that animal, that animal is real and it becomes their friend.'

Thredbo's terrain was ideal for Spalding's program development – not just the vertical and variety most skiers and boarders look for, but moreover, in its potential for adventure – the boulders and trees and creeks.

SEEING RED: *In winter 2006, members of Thredbo Snow Sports gather at Friday Flat before their day on the snow. From two instructors in 1958, by 2006 Thredbo Snow Sports had around 200 instructors throughout the season, growing to 300 during peak periods.*

'There are really beautiful places up there, kids love skiing around trees.'

So do the big kids.

'Thredbo's got the terrain and it tends to attract the real "Aussie go for it" type. It's a mountain that suits that,' Spalding said.

It's also a mountain with a clientele that is keen to improve, people who 'just want to get right into the sport and be as good at it as they possibly can. From a ski school perspective, it's fantastic to have that type of clientele.'

Thredbo is also now dealing with the next generation of snowboarders teaching children as young as four years old to ride a snowboard. As Brad Spalding put it, 'Skiers breed skiers and snowboarders breed snowboarders and that compounds into the new program and then the skill level goes up again because they're starting it at such a young age.'

When Adam Hosie, the current Thredbo Snow Sports manager arrived in the village in 1994 (he'd been through one of Spalding's courses in Austria and spent his first season teaching in Kitzbuhel) a busy day in the children's ski school would have involved 80 or 90 three-to-six-year old children.

'Now we'll have anything up to 250 three-to-six-year-old kids in a day. That gives you an idea of the sort of growth that we've gone through,' Hosie said.

'The school group side of it as an area that has also taken off, in no small part due to the Interschools (snow sports competitions) which exposes kids to snow sports in Australia.'

From the two instructors in 1958 – Erharter and Pfister – Thredbo Snow Sports now has around 200 instructors throughout the season, growing to 300 during school holiday periods.

The Austrian connection endures, even if it has been filtered. In 2006 there were still nine Austrian instructors at Thredbo Snow Sports, but the Arlberg technique is long gone, replaced by an Australian teaching method, devised for the local terrain and the shorter, shaped skis that are so good on it.

'We have instructors now who started skiing in our programs as three-year-olds and now teach,' Brad Spalding said.

'They have never skied on a straight ski, they have gone right through and never made a turn on a straight ski.'

Most of the alpine nations are represented at Thredbo Snow Sports. In 2006, the roster included Austrian, Italian, Norwegian, Dutch, British, American, Canadian, Swiss, German and Spanish/Andorran instructors. Among the Australians were instructors fluent in Cantonese and Japanese.

The glamour of the profession might have infected some skiers in the 1960s, 70s and 80s and even if their careers directed them away from the mountains, the appeal remained.

'We're now getting a lot of people who have finished their working careers and are looking to make a lifestyle choice,' Adam Hosie said.

'I sign employment contracts at the start of each year and the number of people in their late 50s through to late 60s has really grown.

'They're not really all that interested in what they get paid, they're doing it because they want the interaction with a huge diversity of people and the thrill of being able to assist someone to get out on the mountain.

'Probably for some of them, it's the job they always wanted – the glamour and mystique of the ski instructor has maybe stuck with them.'

The teaching process has been enhanced by better equipment, but the surface under the skis and boards has also been crucial in improving it for both teacher and pupil.

'The thing that has helped Thredbo is snowmaking and most importantly, the grooming,' Adam Hosie said.

'With the advent of winch cats, the snow surface is prepared so that it's so much flatter and so much more consistent.

'That makes it much easier for the skier to ski in control – it's not just an easy turning ski, it's the easy turning surface also.'

Over the next few decades, Brad Spalding envisages growth in private, personalised instruction and more sophisticated children's programs.

'Kids are pretty critical; they know what they like. The kids program has to be in tune with everything else that's going on, has to remain fresh and interesting.

'You'll need larger kids' centres, you'll need kids' centres not only for the three-to-six-year-olds that we have now, you'll also need them for the seven-to-14s, maybe themed with indoor education as well as outdoor education.

'Thredbo's in a really good position to do that, to provide those facilities,' Spalding said.

Thredbo Ski Racing Club

Thredbo has astonishing depth in ski racing – as the host of Australia's only alpine World Cup event and as host to some of the world's best ski racers.

'Dick Dusseldorp believed Thredbo had a responsibility to help the sport,' Albert van der Lee said. 'In the first season I was there, 1963, we established the Thredbo Cup which was supposed to be the top race in Australia.

SUMMER RACES: *Paul Reader (left) was an exceptional ski jumper in the nordic tradition (height, distance and form as opposed to acrobatics in modern aerials). Like Charles Anton, he was also one of the Thredbo enthusiasts who enjoyed their skiing so much, they would use the late snow drifts on the upper mountain for summer racing over the Christmas holidays.*

ON THE MAP: *The NSW downhill team (below) for the 1957 State Championships which Thredbo hosted, putting the resort's name on the competitive skiing map. The team is William Davy (at left, wearing No. 5), Tony Mandlick, Geoffrey Hughes, Joseph Steiner and Danny Collman. It was a clean sweep for Collman who won the slalom by 8.2 seconds, the giant slalom by 11.4 seconds and the downhill by 12 seconds.*

'We also established good relations with the Ski Council people (the sport's governing body, later known as the Australian Ski Federation and later still, Ski & Snowboard Australia).'

Van der Lee, Karel Nekvapil and others established the Thredbo Ski Racing Club (TSRC) in 1972, to promote ski racing and training in Thredbo.

But it had a wider purpose, Van der Lee said, 'We especially wanted people who lived in the region to have the opportunity.

'In other words, we tried to turn ski racing from predominantly something for children from well-to-do families in the city to all people from the region. I think we achieved that with the Thredbo Ski Racing Club.'

In addition to its support for ski racing at the grass-roots level, club members who have gone on to ski the Olympics for Australia include David Griff and Kim Clifford (now Kosciuszko

Thredbo's general manager) in 1976 at Innsbruck, Jacqui Cowderoy in 1980 at Lake Placid and most recently Jono Brauer in Torino 2006.

Australian paralympic champions have also had an association with the club, including Michael Milton and Rod Hacon. Thredbo resident Jono Brauer joined the TSRC when he was 11, when he moved to Thredbo with his mother, Judy Lenne. She first ran Café Olga (now known as Altitude 1380) and currently runs Frost Bite at the top of the High Noon Supertrail; the arrangement has worked well for Jono Brauer.

'That's how it all got started for me,' Brauer said. 'I started training full time, right through the winter and was asked to go overseas (with the TSRC squad) when I was 11.

'My development as a skier came from there. All the basic positioning and skiing and training all came from the race club, that's what kicked me off to where I am today.'

The Thredbo Cup

Those who have left their names on the 'Thredbo Cup Women's Amateur Ski Classic' include the two-times Olympic gold medallist and 1966 downhill, giant slalom and combined World Champion, Marielle Goitschel (FRA, 1965) and engraved on the 'Thredbo Cup Men's Amateur Ski Classic' are some of the greatest skiers of their era – Jean-Claude Killy (FRA, 1965), Jimmy Heuga (USA, 1967), Ingemar Stenmark (SWE, 1977) and Steve Mahre (USA, 1979).

Bill (William) Day was the first Australian to leave his name on the men's cup (1963) to be joined by Austrian-born Australian racer Manfred Grabler (1973) and fellow Australian Olympians AJ Bear (1997) and Jono (Jonathon) Brauer (2000, 2001).

Christine Smith who skied for Australia in the 1964 Innsbruck Olympics was the first Australian women's winner (1963, 1964) to be followed by Olympians Sally Rodd (1975), Jenny Altermatt (1976, 1978, 1979, 1981), Jeanette Korten (1996, 1997) and Jenny Owens (1998, 2002).

Australia's first, and until now only, alpine Olympic medallist, Zali Steggall, who won bronze in the slalom at Nagano in 1998, then won the slalom World Championship title at Vail in 1999, left her name on the cup four times (1994, 1995, 1999, 2001).

The White Circus

Was it a landmark event or a financial folly? The 1989 World Cup cemented Thredbo's place on the alpine skiing map, but the debate goes on about its overall value.

The ambition of Kurt Lance and others in the Australian Ski Federation was to run a downhill at Thredbo – something they were to attempt at the internationally sanctioned Australian Bicentennial race meeting in 1988.

In the weeks leading up to that event, the weather was perfect and the snow cover ideal 'then it rained for five days,' Kurt Lance said in an interview at the time. 'And we could see the bloody snow trickling down the hill.'

Some maintain the course was too narrow for alpine skiing's most dangerous event; whether it was the weather or the run, the international team coaches voted to hold a giant slalom event in 1988 and following its success, despite the elements, the International Ski Federation gave Thredbo the right to host slalom and giant slalom World Cup events in 1989.

The World Cups were held on August 12 and 13 in 1989; the first for the season on the men's circuit.

The course preparation was superb and the snow cover better than average but a tremor went through the village when it started to rain on the eve of the first race.

The opening ceremonies began in pouring rain, but then, as the sun started to set, the rain turned to snow as hundreds of skiers gathered at Black Sallees for a massive flare run.

It was as though Thredbo had written the recipe – the weather cleared, the temperature plummeted and the course froze race-hard.

The sun shone for the giant slalom and the forerunner, Australia's first skiing World Cup winner, Malcolm Milne, described the course as 'terrific and fast. Very, very fast.' The speed on the course was best exploited by Lars-Boerje Eriksson who won the giant slalom for Norway. The following day, Austria's Armin Bittner won the slalom. For his second place in both events, Sweden's Ole Christian Furuseth was the Thredbo Cup winner and left Australia as the overall leader in the 1989-90 World Cup.

They were in celebrated company at Thredbo, racing alongside the likes of Pirmin Zurbriggen, Marc Girardelli and Alberto Tomba.

The races were beamed around the world, to an audience the host network, Australia's Nine Network estimated at 300 million people.

For Wayne Kirkpatrick, Kosciuszko Thredbo's managing direc-

WINNERS, GRINNERS: *For his second places in the slalom and giant slalom, Sweden's Ole Christian Furuseth (above) was the leader in the overall FIS Alpine World Cup standings for 1989-90 after the two World Cup events at Thredbo. He was also awarded the Thredbo Cup, which he is holding here.*
In the slalom on the first day of racing, Austrian Gunther Mader (right) pushes himself out of the start gate on Crackenback near Kareela.

tor at the time, that exposure, alongside all the newspaper and magazine space underpinned the value of the event.

'It was an opportunity to unveil Thredbo to the Australian population.' He said they were realistic enough to see they were not going to attract a huge international market. 'But certainly within Australia, it put a stamp of approval and quality on Thredbo. It said, look, it has been substantially improved as a result of all these investments and you can come here in confidence and you can invest in the place.'

There was also the satisfaction in running a successful event. As Kirkpatrick said, 'I know for a fact that FIS (the International Ski Federation) and Hans Gruber who was the man running the men's alpine World Cup at the time were very sincere when they said this was the "best run World Cup" ever.

'It's not just about short-term cash-out, cash-in. It's not just about what it costs.'

But the cost lingers for others. AHL chairman Alan Rydge remembered it as an expensive exercise.

'In those days you know, you run the argument that we were putting skiing in Australia on the international map, and there was an element of that. I mean a lot of people who follow that circuit would not have been aware that you can actually ski in Australia, but at the same time, not a lot of them came back and spent their money.'

Although he had left Thredbo well before the World Cup, Albert van der Lee was succinct in his assessment. 'I thought it was a waste of money, time and effort. It was over the top.' The event director for Thredbo's World Cup, John Kean, had this to say in 1989: 'If you were to ask people to think of ski resorts around the world, they would usually suggest names like Vail and Aspen, Kitzbuhel and Wengen, Whistler and Lake Louise. These are all World Cup venues ... (now) Thredbo can be added to that list.'

Disabled skiing

It all started in the Piano Bar.

Ron Finneran, afflicted by polio at 22 months and left with limited movement in both legs and his right arm, wanted to see what skiing was like.

He spent the winter of 1974 in Thredbo, working as an accounts clerk for Kosciuszko Thredbo.

'I was taken by the sport, it was a bit like a drug for me, I suppose that's similar to us all in the business.

'I wanted to get to the point where I could ski and when I first tried it, all I could try it on was two skis and two poles.'

In that 1974 season he met Thredbo ski patroller Tommy Tomasi who gave him some help and introduced him to some Austrian instructors in the Thredbo Ski School.

They had seen people in their home town, war veteran amputees, skiing with one ski and outriggers. They made Finneran some sketches and he used them as a blueprint to build outriggers. He was mobile.

Finneran spent the 1974-75 northern winter in Canada and the United States and returned to work in Thredbo in 1975, skiing with the outriggers.

'I was invited to attend the first Winter Paralympic Games – in those days it was known as the Winter Olympics for the Disabled and that was held in Ornskoldsvik in Sweden in February 1976. 'I stayed and studied in Sweden for the next two years and returned to Thredbo in 1978.'

By that time, Bruce Abel, a Canadian ski instructor had joined the Thredbo Ski School and he and Finneran decided to form an organisation for disabled skiers.

'He and I got it off the ground, but it was officially ratified in the Piano Bar of the Thredbo Alpine Hotel over quite a few beers with a number of instructors from the Thredbo Ski School – Nick Dean, Rod Dunning, Morris Flutey the ski school supervisor and Arnold Konrad, the ski school director at the time.'

Ron Finneran, Nick Dean and Bruce Abel are still with the organisation.

'We formed what was then known as the Australian Disabled Skiers Federation, Maureen Rupcic was our first secretary, the wife of Thredbo's then service station owner,' Finneran said.

The programs began with annual disabled ski weeks based at the House of Ullr and outside those, individual skiers would meet up with Bruce Abel who would get them up and running through the Thredbo Ski School.

In 1982, the Disabled World Championships were held in Switzerland at Le Diableret; this was the first time Finneran had seen a sit-ski.

Returning from Switzerland, Finneran and the group built the first sit-ski with the help of Thredbo's maintenance crew.

'It was basically a leaf spring with a red plastic Coca-Cola chair attached to it. You know the first person to test run it was Kim Clifford, on the Basin at Thredbo.'

'How'd the test run go, Ron?'

'Kim's still with us.'

Bruce Abel and Nick Dean, who was then also president of the national ski instructor's body, the APSI, took steps to ensure other ski schools were involved.

The ski areas had already given their support. In 1978, Finneran approached Kosciuszko Thredbo to see if the company could arrange for disabled skiers to have some concessions on lifts and lessons.

They, in turn, arranged an invitation for him to meet the Australian Ski Areas Association, the resort operators' group.

'The proposal was put to them and they unanimously offered us lessons and lift tickets free of charge.'

However Finneran saw it as crucial that the disabled skiers make some contribution.

'We chose to say "thanks but no thanks," if we could have 50% off both, that would suit us admirably and that policy, which was put in place by the ASAA back in those days, still remains, every resort in the country supports that.'

AUSTRALIA'S FASTEST: *Michael Milton freeskiing the Bluff – his Thredbo favourites 'all depend on the way the wind has blown.'*

Educating the mountain staff remains important. Each year Disabled Wintersport Australia (DWA) runs clinics with instructors and lift operators, showing them the equipment and creating a 'comfort zone between those supplying the service and those using it.

'We're in our 30th year of operation at Thredbo and the lift crew are absolutely incredible. They make it fun – if a disabled skier is in strife anywhere on the mountain, someone will pop up to help them.

'There is an ethos, a certain special feeling at Thredbo regarding disabled skiers. It includes village regulars, lodge owners, instructors, patrollers, fellow skiers – they are all so very supportive,' Finneran said.

What does disabled skiing do for its participants?

'If you take myself,' Ron Finneran said, 'I had never before been in a position where I could have the wind blowing through my hair – having initiated it myself and being in total control (I use the word "control" loosely here).

'That was the greatest motivating factor for me; it's a primary motivating factor for people with disabilities. To be able to go to the top of a mountain and ski to the bottom unaided is just an enormous rush.'

Beyond the accomplishment of individual skiers, DWA has had significant competitive success.

Michael Milton lost a leg to bone cancer when aged nine; he had skied Thredbo since he was three – his father John Milton was a volunteer Thredbo patroller – and he wasn't going to let the amputation stop him.

'I learnt again when I was nine and lost a leg. Thredbo has always been a part of my skiing and they came on board as a sponsor in 2003 and that has been a major part of my recent success.'

He first represented Australia aged 14, at the Winter Paralympic Games in Innsbruck in 1988. He won slalom in 1992 at Albertville and in that year was also awarded the Order of Australia medal.

In total, Milton has won six gold Paralympic medals, including an unprecedented four gold in a clean sweep of the alpine events at the 2002 Paralympics.

Speed skiing has been his most recent winter pursuit and in that form of the sport, he became the first skier with a disability to break the 200 km/hr barrier and in April 2006, the fastest-ever Australian skier, with a speed of 213.65 km/hr in Les Arcs, France.

The record of 212.26 km/hr was previously held by Cooma farmer Nick Kirschner.

Fire brigade

Before it moved into its current station, the Thredbo Fire Brigade had a small appliance stored in a parking bay under the Mowamba Apartments.

The brigade is now part of the NSW Fire Brigades with up to 15 members retained on stand-by and paid according to their turnouts and training time.

'We provide fire suppression and also provide the primary rescue unit within the area – so we cover motor vehicle accidents and domestic and industrial rescue and we also assist the police and ambulance in backcountry search and rescue,' the brigade's captain and station commander, David Milliken said.

One major challenge for the brigade came in January 2003, when bushfires swept through south-east Australia's alpine region, burning a total area of 2 million hectares.

Thredbo Village was evacuated on January 17, 2003. Euan Diver, deputy captain of the Thredbo Fire Brigade, said the fires reached the back door of the resort, nudging the Funnelweb and Golf Course areas and coming as close as Riverside Cabins.

'We had our two Thredbo units and a strike team of four New South Wales Fire Brigades units set up for property protection,' Diver said.

'We did a couple of back burns in conjunction with the National Parks and Wildlife Service – there were about 12 of us and eight from the NPWS – behind Riverside Cabins and down Funnelweb.

'That was the really interesting one. We cut a two kilometre line down Funnelweb and back burned from that. There was no spotting over those lines.

'I was in and out a bit (not surprising – Euan and Susie Diver's second daughter was born on January 18 – a hot start to life!) but the fire came through on Australia Day.

'It was a much cooler fire higher up and we managed to pull up the main fire in the valley.'

The Thredbo Fire Brigade was also very active in the 1997 road collapse – see page 98.

ON FIRE: *In 2003 (right) fire surrounds Thredbo as the Australian Alps burn; this view is over the Village Green and up-river towards Dead Horse Gap. It's a similar scenario in the 1960s (below) as fire comes close to the village but is kept at bay.*

The chapel

Not everyone is religious, but communities need a cultural and spiritual centre.

Kosciuszko Thredbo's managing director in the 1990s, David Osborn said: 'We saw it as very important – every country town has one,'

Thredbo's chapel was driven by the community, along with the three main religions of the region – Anglican, Roman Catholic and Uniting – but much of the energy was attributed to the Catholic priest at the time, Father Wally Stefanski.

'Father Wally was very charismatic,' Michelle Reichinger said. 'He could get anybody to do anything. It was very hard to say no to Father Wally. He was introduced to skiing when he was the Thredbo priest and he really took to it.

'He'd get skis on and get up that mountain and he'd let them go and he'd go like a bullet. He'd manage to get down – I don't think he had a lot of style but he had a lot of power.

'He was quite extraordinary, he did a lot for Thredbo, he was very sad to leave the area, but he made his mark in Thredbo.

'He was quite an entrepreneur – I think the Polish community put a lot of money into it,' Reichinger said.

He was indeed entrepreneurial; in a previous life Father Wally had been a property developer.

'Kosciuszko Thredbo made a major contribution towards the establishment of the chapel, about $200,000, and Father Wally set about raising the rest,' Osborn said.

'Gerry Gleeson, Adrian Lane and Graeme Herring, who were directors of Kosciuszko Thredbo and Greater Union supported it at a board level, as did Graham Abrahams (Uniting Church) and Harvey Sloan (Anglican).'

Osborn recalled 'some problems with the NPWS in the approvals process for the chapel: "What do you need a church for?" they would ask. We had problems getting the approvals.

'One opening weekend, Father Wally was doing his usual blessing of the snow and the NSW Environment Minister, Chris Hartcher was present.

'As he was addressing the gathering, Father Wally said the plans were going well for the chapel and then announced, unbeknown to any, that "the chapel would be called St Christopher's, after the patron saint of travellers, which just happens to be the name of our Minister for the Environment Chris Hartcher who is here this morning – welcome Chris".'

Osborn asked Father Wally 'how on earth could you do that and he said, "it just came out".

'Whatever, in three days we had our approval and within 12 months the chapel was built,' Osborn said.

Father Wally led a pilgrimage to Rome to have a brick for the chapel blessed by Pope John Paul II, Karol Wojtyla, a fellow Pole whom Father Wally knew.

This might have been enough to tip the naming rights his way. In the end, Thredbo's chapel became known as the Mary MacKillop Chapel within the John Paul II Ecumenical Centre

'One of the earliest services in the chapel was the memorial service following the Thredbo tragedy in 1997.

'There is comfort in rituals and a place like a chapel gives a setting for this. If the chapel wasn't the spiritual heart of Thredbo before the road collapse, it certainly was afterwards,' David Osborn said.

At that service in August 1997, the Thredbo community was joined by the Governor-General, Sir William Deane, Deputy Prime Minister Tim Fischer (Prime Minister John Howard was in hospital at the time) and the Leader of the Opposition, Kim Beazley.

Beazley spoke of 'the beautiful ecumenical service held at the church in Thredbo … It was conducted by Father Wally Stefanski, who did it with great dignity and incorporated all the faiths within it. I would single him out for praise, not only in that regard but also in relation to the efforts that he and others of the clergy were making to comfort the families and to ensure the success of the rescue.

'The people of Thredbo will never forget this. It will be a sadness in that town forever. The fact that a community hall will be built will mean that it is commemorated in an appropriate way, that memory lives on in an appropriate tangible form as well as in the minds of the people who have been concerned and so affected,' (*Hansard*, August 25, 1997).

The road collapse

Nothing tests a community like tragedy.

Around 11.30pm on Wednesday 30 July, 1997, a section of the Alpine Way above Carinya Lodge collapsed. Within seconds Carinya was torn in two, its west wing sliding down the slope, over Bobuck Lane, ploughing into Bimbadeen Lodge causing it to collapse and continue the movement down the slope.

There was one person in Carinya Lodge and 18 people in Bimbadeen. Of these 19 people, 18 died. The sole survivor, Stuart Diver, was located just before dawn on Saturday August 2 and pulled from the rubble late that afternoon.

The causes were complex, but the NSW Coroner found the neglect of the government authorities responsible for the Alpine Way led to the collapse of the road and the consequent landslide.

Bimbadeen was a staff lodge. That meant the people in it were best known by the core of the community, particularly its year-round and longer-term residents and visitors. Friendships and relationships were deep and extensive.

With voices calling for help from the debris, the immediate response of people nearby was to scramble over the site to try and rescue people within it.

Safety is the first principle in any emergency. Members of the local emergency service, the Thredbo Fire Brigade, along with police officers who happened to be staying in the village had to apply it.

It's an uncompromising principle at a time when instinct and emotion plead for compromise, but the site was so unstable, some of the emergency services personnel to be first on scene had to force their friends to stop looking for their friends.

The Thredbo Fire Brigade has dual firefighting and rescue responsibilities and was the first agency on scene.

'It was difficult to size up what had actually happened, it was an odd situation,' Thredbo Fire Brigade captain David Milliken recalled.

'We had people in the building who were still alive at the time and unfortunately passed away not long after our arrival.

'Our role there was a firefighting and also rescue role, as you can imagine, other services came and other personnel from other areas.'

The rescue and recovery operation continued for more than a week and involved hundreds of people.

It is brilliantly documented in *Survival*, the book by Stuart Diver and Simon Bouda and more technically in the June 2000 report of the NSW Coroner.

There are numerous stories that remain untold as part of the tragedy. In some way, it will have affected everyone who has had any connection with Thredbo.

One story revolves around the affect on Kosciuszko Thredbo, its people, the people of the village and their collective response.

Crisis planning and crisis management is now much more significant in corporate Australia, not least because of the Thredbo experience, but as David Osborn said, 'There was no manual. There were no books and even if there was, there was no time to learn.'

Around a third of the company's managers were in Bimbadeen. Despite the agony of their absence, around 5.30 in the morning after the collapse, Osborn, who had driven through the night from Sydney on hearing the news, and the remaining management team met and established their initial response.

They had four basic aims: support the rescue operation; ensure adequate counselling was available for residents and employees; establish communications to at least try to keep pace with the demand for information; and get operations back to normal as quickly as possible.

Andrew Cocks was the primary contact for the police and rescue operation and, along with Euan Diver, worked to get water back into the village – the pumps were under Bimbadeen and they were all gone.

Kim Clifford was in charge of operations, of getting the place working again, and David Osborn and Maureen Roberts handled Thredbo's people and the media.

'Our people just continually pulled things out of hats, the police would ask for something and it would be there, it was an incredibly resourceful response,' Osborn said.

The thirst for information was enormous, so a system was set up where (NSW Police Superintendent) Charlie Sanderson, who was in charge of the rescue operation, would go to Thredboland at Friday Flat each day at 3pm. Anyone who worked or lived in the village was invited to come.

'There was no media. They could ask anything they liked. The first day I reckon there were 600 people, the next day about 300, the next day about 100 and after about five days it just fizzled out – people's need to know what was happening had just dissipated,' Osborn said.

By mid-afternoon on July 31, the basis for counselling sup-

MEMORIES: *This plaque is located at the Thredbo Memorial Community Centre.*

IN MEMORY
OF FAMILY & FRIENDS
WHO DIED IN THE
ROAD COLLAPSE
30th JULY 1997

DI AINSWORTH
JOHN CAMERON
BARRY DECKER
SALLY DIVER
DIANE HOFFMAN
WERNER JECKLIN
OSKAR LUHN
ANDREW McARTHUR
STEVE MOSS
WENDY O DONOHUE
MARY PHILLIPS
AINO SENBRUNS
MIKE SODERGREN
MIM SODERGREN
STEVEN UROSEVIC
COL WARREN
DAVID WATSON
TONY WEAVER

port was established at the Thredbo Alpine Hotel, with counsellors from the Salvation Army, Kosciuszko Thredbo's insurance company, along with the Catholic priest, Father Wally Stefanski and the Uniting Church Pastor Graham Abrahams.

Within the resort, all possibilities were canvassed about its operations, including closing the resort, but the view of the counsellors was that the best strategy for all involved was to try and keep operations as normal as possible.

It was a decision the media couldn't always cope with.

Naturally enough, the national interest was enormous and this led to a media invasion – 10 days of live coverage out of Thredbo.

At times they would run out of things to say.

As much as it has to satisfy the thirst for content, the media has a terrible weakness for cliché, falling for the populist pitch when another angle seems absent. Some within it with limited exposure to the mountains simply subscribe to the theory that snow sports are the domain of the idle rich.

Perhaps with this platform to spring from, some journalists

including ABC-TV's Kerry O'Brien expressed outrage that soon after the collapse people were skiing again at Thredbo. Osborn said: 'Kerry O'Brien tore me apart on the *7.30 Report*, for running the lifts … for some reason he decided on the line that "You're the company, you're heartless, you just want to run the lifts, all these people are dead, how can you run your lifts?"'

'The answer was simple – because that's what the psychologists told me was the best thing to do – "let people go for a ski, keep things as normal as possible".'

The external interest was reflected in the web statistics. Even though the internet had nothing like the penetration it now has, hits on Thredbo's site went from around 10,000 a day to 90,000.

Australia wanted to help. Several different relief funds sprang up and it soon became apparent this could become fractured and chaotic.

The funds were rolled into one with AHL chairman Alan Rydge managing the Thredbo Relief Fund. Kosciuszko Thredbo diverted 10% of revenue from the remaining winter season into the fund.

Osborn handled communications with the help of Ian Foster, the Thredbo Chamber of Commerce president. 'We wanted it to be seen as a village response rather than a Kosciuszko Thredbo response,' Osborn said.

'Really, you can't predict the kinds of questions that you are going to get in those uncontrolled media interviews when you're sitting behind a table with a policeman and a couple of other people and there are 40 or 50 journalists in the room firing off questions.

'But again, we just had some principles – to project corporate values of honesty and integrity, hiding nothing and cooperating with the coroner.'

Particularly in the early days, a nagging concern for the key people in Kosciuszko Thredbo remained: could they in some way have contributed to the road collapse?

Because of a change in insurers, the company had two full risk assessments completed by external experts in the two years prior to the road collapse.

'Nowhere in any of those risk management studies did it ever mention anything about the road collapsing,' Osborn said.

'So there was nothing we knew about that we hadn't done. That was pretty important.

There were a lot of people who wanted to point blame.

'The road had moved, the water main had fractured and there was water pouring everywhere and the question, ultimately, became what happened first – did the road move and break the pipe or did the pipe break and saturate the road fill.

'As we now know, the road moved first, but the first people on site and particularly the National Parks people were very keen to point to the water main and say, "Oh that's what's caused it".

'They continued to say that and continued to try and shift the blame and not want to accept any of the responsibility.

'That was terribly hard to combat – we weren't going to blame anybody but we weren't going to accept any blame either until a lot more work had been done.'

The stalemate with the NPWS continued through 1997. As they started to look at the next winter season, Kosciuszko Thredbo's sub-lessees were becoming increasingly concerned – they wanted somebody to tell them that it was safe to occupy their lodge.

The problem was, the Alpine Way collapsed because there was uncompacted fill in the gullies on the slope it was carved into and this fill remained in a number of areas.

'There was a lot of monitoring equipment in there,' Osborn recalled, 'and the gullies weren't shifting, but Kosciuszko Thredbo was under a lot of pressure to say whether or not they were safe and we couldn't really say that when the fill was still there.

'In any event, it was not our road. It was up to the NPWS to say that it was safe and we did not have their monitoring data – their lawyers were not letting that information out at that time.

'What we'd been saying to the NPWS was, "Just get rid of that fill – stop fiddling around" but they were just doing little things, they didn't want to do anything significant because they didn't want to acknowledge that they should have done something before.'

The issue was brought to a head when Osborn called a press conference at the Wesley Centre, in Pitt Street, in the heart of Sydney.

'We announced that we had told 17 lodges in Thredbo not to open for the following (1998) winter because we'd been unable to get any guarantees on their behalf from the NPWS about the safety or otherwise of the road.

'It caused an absolute storm. Thredbo was back on the front page, but it forced the NPWS to respond.

'We were simply saying, "Just dig up the fill and take it away" and when they eventually did, it took 20 or 30 trucks and four or five front end loaders about a month to get rid of it all.

'At the time, a lot of sub-lessees criticised us for that, but really, we had to corner the NPWS to either get the road in such a condition that somebody could say it was safe to sleep in those lodges, or get them to say it wasn't safe and that people should not have been staying there.

'As soon as that process was started, we were able to call another press conference and say "OK, we withdraw our recommendation for those lodges to close."

'From that point on, sub-lessees knew where they stood and something was actually being done – the NPWS announced they were going to fix the road and the NSW Government

FREE RANGING: *The signature giant granite tors, sentinels on the Ramshead Range above Thredbo. They are one of the natural drawcards for Thredbo's visitors and its residents.*

made funds available for that. Reconstruction started the following summer (1998-99).'

The immediate objective following the road collapse was to look after Thredbo's people but a parallel objective began to emerge – to manage and restore the perception of Thredbo as a brand.

After the last rescue workers left, Thredbo residents faced the long task of rebuilding and apart from the emotional trauma, they also had to confront the commercial devastation that threatened their business, their livelihood.

There was also a fundamental fiduciary responsibility, as Reg Bryson, who at the time was with Kosciuszko Thredbo's advertising agency, the Campaign Palace put it, 'Kosciuszko Thredbo was (and is) the wholly owned subsidiary of a public company – Amalgamated Holdings Limited.

'They therefore had a fiduciary duty to protect their business, the shareholders' investment and the 650-odd business operators and sub-lessees within the village itself.'

Leading into winter 1998, bookings were down and press coverage had been essentially negative.

David Osborn said: 'We had two goes at delivering what I called the "ultimate safety and reassurance" message, but our studies were showing each time we tried to tell people Thredbo was safe, the perception that it was unsafe increased,'

It was Darren Wilson, a clinical psychologist who had been part of the counselling team that cracked it.

'He said, "I know what's going on, I reckon you're reminding people – people have got some bad memories with what happened, it's slowly mixing up in their minds with all the good memories. What you're doing by telling them it's safe is just reminding them, you're bringing the negative stuff to the surface. I reckon the best thing you can do is just go and behave as you've always behaved."

'And what that meant in Thredbo's case was going back and running really irreverent ads,' Osborn said.

'I never told the board what we were going to do because I didn't think I could convince them – they always looked sideways at Thredbo's ads anyway – so we ran a series of irreverent Thredbo ads and the perceptions of safety went up, we never mentioned safety, never said a word about it.'

Together with Reg Bryson and his team at the Campaign Palace, a series of advertisements were developed which returned to Thredbo's established advertising style – edgy, irreverent and humorous.

Bryson said the research from the agency 'matched the message from the village – the people that died would not like to see change, they liked Thredbo for how it is.'

The Nagano Winter Olympics in February 1998 provided a platform to create and televise a series of advertisements in that traditionally irreverent style.

'We sent one guy with a Handy Cam and our writer and our art director and we roughly discussed the concept and what they could do before they went up there [to Nagano].

'We wanted a whole series of little 15-second commercials somehow talking about Thredbo relating to the Nagano Olympics; nothing was really scripted or finalised.

'They went up there and they came back with a series of about 10 ads and they became a talking point of the Nagano Olympics because they were so funny.

'Like the one with two Japanese girls standing in the snow. The copywriter would walk up with a Thredbo microphone and say, "Excuse me girls?" and the Japanese girls would turn around and smile and say, "Yes?" and he said, "Which snowball has the best snow? The snowball from Nagano?" and he threw the snowball at one girl "or the snowball I brought from Thredbo?" and he threw that and hit the other girl and the girls said, "We think Thredbo's snowball is the best snow." And he'd say, "Thanks girls".'

The campaign won the global tourism and resort marketing advertising award for the year in New York.

It also worked on the ground; Thredbo's summer revenue grew 4% that year and its winter market share grew 1% in 1998.

'Thredbo did well,' David Osborn said.

'It started off with 600 people in counselling and two years later, had one.

'Its visitor numbers were badly knocked around the year the road collapsed, but within a year or two, those numbers were back.

'If Thredbo was a person, it was a person who had been through hard times and had gained maturity and understanding and depth and history.

'Maybe that's a terrible way to talk about something like that but I think that's how Thredbo came out of it at the other end.'

Community centre

Before the Thredbo Memorial Community Centre was built, Thredbo's pre-schoolers were a vagrant bunch; gathering in lodges such as Sequoia or, outside winter, at Friday Flat.

'We needed a focus for the people who lived here,' Ann Koeman said. 'We didn't have a school, we didn't have a library, we didn't have any of the normal things that a community would have.

'Even a small country town would have a pre-school and a library, somewhere where community gatherings would happen,' she said.

Ann Koeman first came to Thredbo in 1961 and came to stay in 1962; she and her husband Cees Koeman celebrated the 40th year of their lodge, Kasees, in 2006.

From the early 1970s, a ball was held once or twice a year in the hotel dining room. It was a feature on the social calendar for the local people.

'We decided if we were going to have those kinds of things, we'd have to have something to do it for and the logical solution was a community hall, even though the community was very small at that time,' Ann Koeman said.

'So we had those events once or twice a year and anything else the local community raised money for went into that fund … it wasn't enough to build a hall, but it was a start.

'Of course, the unfortunate circumstance was, when the landslide happened and people wanted something to unite them, that's when the community hall finally got under way – with help from government – and that's where the funds ended up.'

The result, she said, '… has been absolutely wonderful, particularly for the kids.'

If we have a request for weddings, we can have receptions in the hall and we use it for music festivals and the golf club uses it.'

Ann Koeman also got the library she was always after. In the early days, the closest library was in Cooma, which had a mobile library that would travel as far as Jindabyne.

Now the library is 'in pretty good shape upstairs and the kids have a wonderful time with the early learning centre downstairs.

The library books come from donations, from ski clubs and staff who are moving on.

'They leave boxes and boxes of books. I don't really catalogue them, but we have sorted them into fiction and health and craft and kids' stuff.

VILLAGE HEART: *A community centre was the ambition of Thredbo's residents from the village's earliest days. It has come to fruition and contains a pre-school and a library and creates a focus for the village and its visitors.*

'It's all run on an honesty system and is only accessible when the early learning centre is open downstairs, but it's working well,' Ann Koeman said.

'It's a great thing for the village,' Michelle Reichinger said. 'The community centre was a long time coming. When we were involved with the pre-school here, the one thing we really thought we needed, more than a school, was a community centre.

'We didn't have anywhere that the children could play, outside our own homes and probably the Bistro which really wasn't suitable as it was licensed premises and they probably shouldn't have been there.

'The community centre really gave Thredbo its heart and soul for the locals.'

The project was supported by both the NSW and Federal Governments. On the same day in Federal Parliament that Kim Beazley was speaking about the memorial service, Prime Minister John Howard announced the Federal Government would 'contribute $100,000 to allow work to commence on a planned Thredbo community hall.

'The Thredbo Recovery Coordination Committee has recommended the community hall be built to help the village cope with the grieving and as a project to unite the village in a cause to keep alive the strong community spirit and to focus energies.

'The community hall, I understand, has been a priority and a fundraising focus of residents for many years. I understand that plans were complete but that construction had been delayed for financial reasons.

'The hall will be located near the church at the western end of the village. It will house Thredbo's only year-round pre-school facility; be a venue for social, sport and recreational groups; and generally offer the residents an informal, personal place,' (*Hansard*, August 25, 1997).

Ironically, the location, like the community centre itself, had on once seemed so distant.

The then Deputy Prime Minister Tim Fischer officially opened the centre and Ann Koeman gave a speech as a community representative. She remembers commenting that, 'Where that site is now, we thought it was so far out of the village – that gives you an idea how small the village was when we first started raising the funds.'

Images, events and entertainment

Thredbo is eclectic in the accurate sense – comprised of a diversity of elements – but it is unified by the form of its natural environment and in its art, appearance, events and entertainment.

Thredbo's sculptures spring up in surprising style, scattered with extraordinary creativity through the village. They range from the warm and natural *Wombat's Throne*, a work in wood by Edward Hayes at Valley Terminal, to the *Grey Kangaroo* in bronze by Silvio Apponyi, by the playground on the Village Green.

In more abstract form, *Inside Space* in the Village Square, a creation of Japanese-born sculptor Toshiaki Izumi is a representation of harmony with nature. It commemorates the years when Lend Lease operated the resort.

Acquisitive art and sculpture competitions have been used to increase the collection, although some pieces have been donated.

Art in other forms is at the heart of the village experience. Thredbo's Chamber of Commerce president, Ian Foster, puts the success of Thredbo's jazz and blues festivals down to their suitability for the kind of people who like to visit Thredbo outside winter. The range of venues in Thredbo is also important.

'We don't have big venues; we don't have venues where you get thousands of people … in Thredbo they're sitting right up close with nowhere to go.

'It's the same for the performers; you really see a relationship developing over the weekend between the audience and the performers as individuals but also the performers working with each other,' Foster said.

'Some of the best gigs you see in a music festival will be late on the Sunday evening when they've had the whole weekend to get warmed up and the performers are all becoming comfortable with each other and sitting in on jam sessions. 'There are some extraordinary performances at this stage where you have people up on stage playing off each other and really enjoying themselves – you can just see it, they're having way more fun than anyone else in the room and the audience is already going berserk.'

International performers share the feeling – some play at music festivals at larger mountain resorts in North America, Aspen for example, but Foster said what strikes them about Thredbo is the 'intimacy of the village and its unique atmosphere.

MUSIC IN THE MOUNTAINS: *The accordionist sets the scene for après in the 1950s (above). Candlelight Lodge's Kornel Deseo is leaning against the fireplace. In 2003, the music rolls along at the Jazz Festival with Dan Barnett on vocals, Sam Rollings on guitar and Greg Royal on double bass.*

'People from all over the world come into Thredbo and feel this vibe over the weekend and it's quite extraordinary.'

The Village Square also comes into its own during the festivals – it's a big enough outdoor space to fit 800 to 1000 people but still retain that feeling of intimacy with the village buildings surrounding it.

During the Snowy Ride, a huge motorcycle event Thredbo hosted in late spring, they've had acts as big as Jimmy Barnes and The Angels playing in the Village Square.

'That'll possibly help the festivals step up to another level – it gives us a larger performance space but still retains that intimacy that enhances it in Thredbo,' Foster said.

Timing is everything, no more so than in the festivals. There are more than 50 music festivals on the calendar throughout Australia, virtually one for every weekend, so it was

Thredbo's foresight and good fortune to take a place on that calendar before it became crowded.

'We managed to wear a groove in the festival calendar before it became *a la mode* to run a music festival,' Foster said.

'Over the last 10 years they've been popping up all over the place and there's a limited number of weekends in the calendar.'

The chamber has a role in creating a bridge between the businesses of the village and their landlord, Kosciuszko Thredbo, and it has also been instrumental in creating summer business for the resort, particularly through events and festivals.

The range has been extraordinary, including the world music festival, a health and lifestyle event based on aerobic style activity, triathlon and even a Shakespeare Festival.

'They have lasted anywhere from three to five or six years, but we've always had a policy that they have to reach a point where they're self-sustaining and if they don't, then we don't continue to support them,' Foster said.

'The Jazz Festival became self-sustaining really quite quickly, and so did Blues – the third year out it was actually paying for itself, by that I mean it wasn't costing the Chamber of Commerce anything to run in the end.'

The festivals have a dual role; to entertain people in the village and to show them what it is like outside winter; this in turn creates awareness.

'If you went out and tried to sell Thredbo in summer to people who'd spent the last 20 summers at the beach, they'd just look at you and wonder what you were talking about,' Foster said.

'But if you build a legion of loyal followers who've been here in summer and know what it's about, you get them talking about what the place has to offer and what a special environment it is.'

Getting Thredbo's message out has had a varied past. Advertising wasn't a new phenomenon when Thredbo was established, but its emergence and spectacular growth in many ways paralleled the resort's, not least because of the parallel growth of television as a medium.

Until the 1980s, Thredbo followed conventional paths in its advertising – skiing magazines and local newspapers; print was the medium, with perhaps some radio exposure alongside.

A young Wayne Kirkpatrick sought to change that, but it didn't happen as quickly as he hoped. It was advertising that initially drew Kirkpatrick to Thredbo, but as a practitioner rather than a consumer.

He worked for an agency that was part of the Interpublic Group that had Thredbo as a client. Kirkpatrick became so attracted to the resort, he moved to Thredbo with his wife and young son in 1979. He intended to simply spend the season skiing, but found work doing some publicity and promotion and was appointed marketing director. In 1984 he became managing director.

With his marketing background, Kirkpatrick sought to steer Thredbo in a different direction from its engineering pioneers. One of his primary aims was to alter its image. He saw advertising as an opportunity to do this, but it didn't work entirely as he first intended.

He approached a fledgling agency in Sydney called the Campaign Palace. At this point, the Palace had a small client list but it was making a name for itself in creativity with a campaign for Sydney's Taronga Zoo and later through advertisements such as Computer Socks, No Knickers and Antz Pantz. 'Wayne said he wanted us to create one of those famous ads,' said Reg Bryson, who became chairman and chief executive of the Campaign Palace and handled Thredbo's advertising for two decades.

'But we did some research and found Thredbo had the worst image possible. It was Double Bay on ice and not

The logo

There have only been four logos for Kosciuszko Thredbo in its 50 years – remarkable continuity given the importance of its image and the pressure to keep it to a contemporary design. The first came from the Kosciuszko Chairlift and Thredbo Hotel Syndicate, a simple graphic which located the resort and its facilities, next came the stylised 'KT' of Kosciuszko Thredbo, which was followed by the all-seasons skier/wildflower/mountain logo of Thredbo Alpine Village and, most recently, the sketch-style Thredbo, topped by a simple mountain peak.

AUSTRALIA'S NEWEST SKI AREA. THE CRUISER AT THREDBO.

many people identified with that set … the village and the mountain were not user-friendly.

'So we went back to Thredbo and said, "You can't have a television commercial." And Wayne said, "Why the … not"?'

'And we said, "because it won't do the job … what we need to say you can't say in 30 seconds." So he said, "Well what do you suggest?" and we said, "You've got to write a book".'

Bryson managed to convince Kirkpatrick that for Thredbo to grow and improve its visitor numbers, they needed to come up with a comprehensive guide that could start to redefine Thredbo's identity and give it some appeal among new skiers.

'We were very conscious of the market in Australia not growing, despite the increasing affluence of Australians,' Kirkpatrick said.

They created the 32-page booklet titled *Thredbo Alpine Village, the First Resort for First Time Skiers*. It took a snow holiday back to its basics, explained what was involved in learning to ski and explained what it would cost.

'That book became world famous, we told people we'd rather make them happy than poor, that we'd cut costs not corners. We told them what things would cost and that gave them a point of perspective,' Bryson said.

IMPRESSIONS: *Canadian artist Brent Lynch created a series of posters for Thredbo; some with a distinctive border that became the trim on staff uniforms. This one introduced the Cruiser when the chairlift replaced the duplex Merritts T-bars in 1995.*

'We explained all about the equipment and packing tips. What do you do about getting fit? Nothing. There's no need for weeks of special ski exercises at the beginner level … it's a holiday, not hard work.

'It proved you could position Thredbo in a different way with different appeal,' Bryson said.

The book was updated and revised and retained a strong place in Thredbo's marketing over the following years. Visitor numbers grew and this in part helped provide the foundation and confidence to embark on the ambitious developments of the late 1980s and early 1990s.

It was one thing to convince beginners that skiing was an easy sport to learn; it became an even simpler argument when there was a facility as simple and accessible as Friday Flat to learn it on.

Ironically, it probably wasn't until after Kirkpatrick left that Thredbo started to get the snappy commercials he had originally sought.

Thredbo was given access to Amalgamated Holdings' Greater Union cinemas for its commercials and there were some landmarks among them.

A film crew was sent to Thredbo and Bryson recalled them returning the material to Thredbo's marketing manager at the time, Barry Atkins, whose response was, 'See if you can do anything with it but if your recommendation is burn it, well, I totally understand because I've seen it all.'

'They were typical film-types,' Reg Bryson said, 'They didn't have a clue about the resort,' so the Campaign Palace turned the material on its head and created what it called the 'Wanker's Ad' for Thredbo.

Carnival week

A significant change in virtually every alpine resort in Australia and many around the world is the movement of staff out of resorts.

A range of forces is at play. Alpine villages have limited bed numbers and there is a commercial priority to make them available to visitors or for development. Also, as the resorts mature, staff seek more permanent dwellings in towns nearby to raise families or simply as a contrast to life in the resort. It changes the village dynamic. Young, single staff in the 1960s, 70s and 80s lived in the village and would often play harder than many of the guests, providing a vibrant backbone for any village event.

In Thredbo, carnival week was an event that celebrated spring and the end of the season, but it faded when the staff started to move out of the village.

'The creativity coming out of this one little village was just amazing, it was a really fun time,' Michelle Reichinger recalled. 'We had body painting, a billycart derby, rubber duck racing down the river, fancy dress, tug of war over the river and rugby on the Village Green.

'Everybody decorated their businesses and lodges and they'd get around in fancy dress during the week, it was a unique thing to be involved with,' she said.

FORMULA NONE: *Searching for speed in the billycart derby, a feature of Thredbo's carnival week program.*

'There was just so much creative energy – people came down here as a bar tender and you'd find out they had all these other skills and amazing abilities. When you pooled them, you came up with these amazing creative concepts.'

'It won a gold award at Cannes (International Advertising Festival). We actually got a picture of a jumbo jet virtually landing in a paddock and it said, "Touchdown Thredbo". We got that exact voice, the Peter Stuyvesant voice and it went on "Every night is Saturday night, that is the way of Thredbo",' Bryson said.

'A lot of people thought it was serious to start with, but at the end, the voice-over just paused and said, "Well, who cares what these wankers smoke. Ski Thredbo, you'll like it".

'The audiences were stunned and people were going away saying, "You've got to go to the cinema to see this ad".

'That started us on a whole genre of television commercials that Thredbo became famous for,' Bryson said.

Fame is one thing, but as Bryson saw when he created the beginner's guide, it will fizzle without substance; service and facilities are crucial to underpin the offering.

Thredbo's bars have always had a healthy following – from the uni-style toga parties in the Keller to the locals gathering in the Bistro and the après skiers enriching their day in the Schuss Bar.

The Hotel's Piano Bar or as it now known, the Lounge Bar was a place for guests to gather and contemplate or celebrate their reunions. In the Austrian tradition, ski instructors would perform their *schuhplattling* or slap dancing. Rudi's, Bernti's, the Black Bear, the T-bar, Alpenhorn and the House of Ullr have always had a following.

Higher on the mountain, Kareela Hutte once hosted nightlife and this now goes higher still at the Eagles Nest restaurant. Restaurants have also had increasing importance. In many ways Thredbo restaurants have followed a similar path, in terms of variety and quality, to restaurants in Australia's larger cities.

In 1980, Noni Plewes and her husband Ron opened Ronnies restaurant in the lodge they had at the time, Snowgoose.

'We ran Ronnies for three years, it was good – there weren't too many restaurants around at that time, Bernti's was very good, and Rudi's, but they were more restaurants within lodges,' Noni Plewes said.

In those days, the main role of the restaurant in the village was to feed house guests in an early sitting and then, around 8pm, open for a la carte dining in a second sitting.

After a few years with Ronnies, the Plewes moved to Canberra to the Charcoal restaurant, a favourite among politicians and the national capital's elite.

STAYING COOL: *Thredbo skiers (below) take a break for refreshment at the snow bar at the top of Crackenback in the early 1960s, while Daniel Talliana (above left) shakes a cocktail behind the bar at Alpenhorn in 2004.*

Accomplished with flare

In the lead-up to the 2000 Sydney Olympics, the Olympic Torch was taken on a spectacular journey around Australia. On September 7, 2000, eight days before the games began in Sydney, the torch left Canberra and travelled through Cooma, Berridale and Jindabyne before arriving in Thredbo. Sasha Nekvapil (who represented Czechoslovakia at the 1948 St Moritz Winter Olympics) carried the torch up the lift and a flare run with around 500 skiers and snowboarders escorted the flame down the Crackenback Supertrail.

The four torchbearers they escorted were Olympians Kim Clifford (Innbsruck 1976) and speed skater Phil Tahmindjis (Calgary 1988, Albertville 1992, and Lillehammer 1994) along with Berridale butcher Gordon Jenkinson and the survivor of the road collapse, Stuart Diver.

With the flame back in the village, the final runner was to take it to the Village Green.

The identity of that runner was being kept a secret, but the village got a hint of what was to come when Frank Prihoda was seen running through town in the days leading up to the event.

He conceded he did a bit of jogging for practice. The giveaway came when 'one day I took a hammer and ran, I wanted to know how it felt if you carried something.

'I was famous, a reporter saw it and then he called Channel 7 and he filmed it, nobody cared about the real thing; "Oh, he's carrying a hammer" they'd say.'

Prihoda's selection was natural – as well as being Thredbo's oldest resident, he had represented Australia as a skier at the 1956 Winter Olympics in Cortina, Italy.

He recalled the day of the torch relay in Thredbo as 'the worst day of the whole season; rain, wind and sleet but there was this enormous mood.

'About 3000 people came and witnessed it and they were all very much in it, you know, they braved the elements and they showed great appreciation of what was happening.

'I had the honour of the last leg and lighting the cauldron and I took off, I started jogging along and took off at the supermarket and then 200 metres or 150 metres along I had to walk for a bit.

'Then down the hill I started jogging again and there was a throng of people, it was a great experience in hindsight,' Prihoda said.

Thredbo lends itself perfectly to flare runs, because its slopes are so easily viewed from the village.

A formal record for a flare run on snow was set in 1998, on the first anniversary of the road collapse, when a *Guinness Book of Records* record was set at 702. This record has since been broken.

Other world records include the world's biggest snowball, which was claimed to have been rolled together at Thredbo, or the endurance skiing record, which was claimed by Nick Willey when he skied for 202 hours and one minute – close to eight days at Thredbo in September 2005. The previous record was 168 hours. Willey estimated he skied about 1150 km and travelled up Thredbo's Easy Does It and Gunbarrel chairs 916 times as part of a campaign that raised around $160,000 for asbestos cancer research.

NIGHT LIGHTS: *Thredbo held the world record for a flare run – 702 skiers in 1998.*

They returned to build the Pond Apartments, near the Village Green and from 1996 to 2005, they ran Credo, above the Thredbo River and near the Riverside Cabins. There was a transformation during that era.

When they started, one of the Plewes' main challenges was to source high quality, fresh produce on a reliable basis.

'We were the first restaurant in the whole region to win an award. We could have almost bought an aeroplane with the freight we used to bring in,' Noni Plewes said.

'We used to bring in lobsters from Perth, scallops and oysters from Adelaide, mud crabs and barramundi from Darwin and we'd get beef from the Darling Downs.

'We used to employ a broker to source the best product and we'd pay the freight down.'

A decade later, the systems are in place to source produce much more simply and much of that is the function of competition.

'There's a lot more competition now at the better end,' she said, 'It (the competition) is very good, very healthy; it keeps people going at a high level.

'The calibre of chef and the calibre of produce now is stunning. The hotel, for example, had fantastic comments coming out of it this year (2006). Now that I'm out of it, people are more open to giving me their opinions.'

The hotel's Cascades Restaurant was named Australia's best Casual/Family Dining option in the 2006 Australian Hotels Association national awards.

In a place like Thredbo, Noni Plewes said, 'It's not just about the food, it's about the wine and the ambience and the quality of the staff, the service has to be good and has to be friendly … in Thredbo, you needed waiting staff who are friendly.'

NIGHT LIFE: *Après ski is less formal in a new century, but in venues like the Keller Bar, it is still at the heart of a winter in the mountains. Here Thredbo Snow Sports instructors Amy Cambridge (front left) and Rochelle Griffiths show their style.*

Credo won numerous awards, including the best restaurant in country NSW to have a wedding. Having sold the business at Credo in 2005, the weddings are one thing Noni Plewes said she missed and they are events Thredbo has become well known for.

She claimed to have been Thredbo's first bride. 'When Ron and I got married here 25 years ago, they turned the Piano Bar into a church for me,' she said.

Perhaps her own wedding in the setting gave her an understanding of the pleasure it could bring others. 'I loved my brides. It's a great occasion, it's happy – mostly happy – if the bride was a little bit stressed it was my job to make her not so stressed.

'I used attend every bride show in Australia. I benefited, but in the long term, the village benefited too. The weddings kept Credo going on a year-round basis.

'The fact that Thredbo is equidistant to Melbourne and Sydney was great (for weddings) and that it is close to Canberra – we get a lot of Canberra brides.

'You know Perth was our fourth-biggest source of weddings, people who had met in Thredbo or got engaged in Thredbo, had some connection with Thredbo,' Plewes said. 'I really miss the interaction but I miss my brides terribly. I had hundreds of brides and I only had one bridezilla.'

Beyond the ski runs

Thredbo's potential beyond the ski runs and also beyond winter was always integral in its appeal and in motivating its pioneers. The natural qualities of the area surrounding it and the heritage of those that came before were also vital.

Dick Dusseldorp immediately recognised Thredbo's potential beyond winter. In part his enthusiasm was motivated by a belief that the Alpine Way connecting the resort with Victoria would have been sealed sooner than it was, but he nevertheless remained the driver behind facilities such as the golf course and the tennis courts and the principle that a chairlift should operate all year round.

His enthusiasm must have been shared by those Europeans that first settled Thredbo who would have spent summer in the mountains in their place of birth, or known of the tradition.

'The summer potential I considered to exceed that of the winter. Winter is limited in the Australian Alps, summer is unique,' Dusseldorp said.

The all-seasons passion for the mountains by many of the early club members should also be recognised, as they saw the scope for the walking and the fishing beyond winter.

Albert van der Lee, Kosciuszko Thredbo's managing director from the early 1960s to 1984 oversaw the development of many of the non-skiing facilities.

His boss, Dick Dusseldorp, had toured around all the ski areas in Australia 'and he realised that none of the others had the position Thredbo had, he saw that it was uniquely placed for summer use.'

With the surety of running a chairlift all year round, they then went about creating some walking tracks.

'People don't really pay for them, but you must have something for them to do on the mountain,' van der Lee said. 'So we made a trail called Merritts Track from the top of the chairlift to the village, through some unique country with the help of the (Kosciuszko National Park) rangers.

'There were other walking tracks established in the area and of course, ultimately, the walking track to Mt Kosciuszko, which was put in by the parks service, apart from the section in the Thredbo lease area – that was paid for by the company. Walking has become tremendously popular in the summer,' van der Lee said.

'People are fishing the rivers, white water rafting has slowly become established – we were nibbling away at all those things.'

Another important factor was the appeal of the village – mountain villages can look like construction sites in the sum-

RANGE RIDING: *Skier Ian Morris (above) heads out on the Ramshead Range with Victoria's highest peak, Mt Bogong and the high plains in the background with a full winter cover, while in summer, a mountain biker (left) crosses the Crackenback Supertrail.*

mer, particularly in their developing years. It needed to look groomed and attractive. 'For a long time we had muddy car parks and so on,' van der Lee recalled.

The golf course was built in the 1970s along with the tennis courts and even a bowling green. The bowling green was on the Village Green – that whole area was drained and flattened – it was there for two years, but there was insufficient interest in bowling so that was reinstated as a Village Green. One of the more recently installed facilities was the alpine slide, the Thredbo Bobsled, something to appeal to younger visitors who may have been looking for some activity but didn't necessarily see themselves as golfers, fishers or tennis players.

Many of those younger visitors have also been involved with the emergence of mountain biking.

Colin Battersby pinpoints Thredbo's hosting of the Australian National Mountain Bike Championships in 1992 as the watershed. Through his business, Raw NRG, he runs three or four major races each year, including the Australian Interschool Mountain Bike Championships, but he said there are plenty of people who visit to go downhill mountain biking, in much the same way they do when they go skiing or boarding – take the chairlift up and ride the mountain bike down.

The same appeal that Thredbo's slopes have for skiers and snowboarders translates to mountain bikers. From the top of the Kosciuszko Express chairlift, they can get a downhill ride of four to six km, depending on the trail they choose.

Battersby believes there is a significant crossover between skiers and snowboarders and mountain bikers 'particularly boarders, probably because of their age, but there's also plenty of skiers. People who come to the mountains in winter, they're more likely to come in the summer.'

This translates across the village; winter visitors who went on to invest in apartments or even club lodge memberships became summer enthusiasts.

'People started to look at Thredbo as an alternative for a holiday and not just for winter use,' Albert van der Lee said. 'Having the apartment anyway, they would come down on the school holidays and enjoy it. And then their children of course continued the tradition.'

In the 1990s, Kosciuszko Thredbo employed a marketing manager specifically to drive summer business.

AFTER THE SNOW: *The showy rice flower or Kosciuszko Rose (below) blooms in the mountains while fly fisher Wayne Dixon (right) casts into the mountain waters of the Thredbo River.*

Wendy O'Donohue, who was a victim of the road collapse, had a brief not to touch winter marketing. 'She would take her holidays in winter or run media trips or give talks in the hotel about summer in Thredbo,' David Osborn, the managing director at the time said.

'We saw we could offer an alternative to the summer beach holiday. We also saw an ageing population, some of whom would want a sea change but others who would want a tree change,' Osborn said.

Improving the art in the village and giving people more to do with facilities such as the Thredbo Bobsled and Thredbo Leisure Centre meant they would stay longer.

'Wendy pushed the events; the Jazz Festival was in place but blues and world music were established under Wendy. 'She was the product champion, she ensured the walking paths were maintained and summer got its place in the annual maintenance expenditure; she had a very good relationship with the people of the village and great people skills as a facilitator.'

Thredbo people admire all its seasons. Frank Prihoda, its oldest resident, wonders why the question is even put.

'Everybody should know that Thredbo's the best place in Australia to live. We have good weather, we have lovely summers, we get it warm and hot at times but it nearly always cools down substantially during the night.'

What's in a name?

It is generally agreed that the names Thredbo, Bredbo and probably Byadbo are of Aboriginal origin, although their original form and meaning are unclear.

Flavia Hodges, director of Macquarie University's Asia-Pacific Institute for Toponymy (placename derivation) said she was aware of a claim that the ending '-by,' which comes from the Scandinavian placename element '-by,' meaning 'settlement,' was applied to Thredbo but believes this is highly unlikely.

'Dr Harold Koch of the Australian National University has looked into Aboriginal-origin placenames of the Monaro, but is not able to assign a meaning to the apparently common element found in both these names (Thredbo and Bredbo) and in Byadbo.' Hodges said the consensus view was that the names are Aboriginal in origin.

The close match of the names had some interesting implications. When a post office was opened in Thredbo in 1958, the Postmaster General's department insisted it be called Crackenback Post Office, to avoid confusion between the existing town of Bredbo and the new settlement at Thredbo. (Sponar, p163)

The name of the post office didn't endure, but the PMG was proven right at least once in its anticipation of the confusion that might follow.

The story goes that a group of northern hemisphere ski instructors, heading south for their first Australian winter, got off the bus in Bredbo, the small wayside town on the Monaro Highway between Canberra and Cooma, and wondered where the lifts were.

As Australia becomes more concerned about its water resources, he pointed to its abundance in Thredbo as another local asset.

'We are blessed with water. If it rains in the region, it rains in Thredbo. It may not rain in Jindabyne but it rains here and it may not rain in Khancoban, but we catch it … that's a blessing. These days it's a great blessing,' Prihoda said.

Ian Foster, who runs Lantern Apartments as well as being the Chamber of Commerce president put it like this: 'The village itself has a charm, but that in itself isn't enough. It's the amazing situation of being in the heart of the Kosciuszko National Park, surrounded by wilderness on three sides.

'I find that quite exciting – you can ride up the chairlift, strap on a pair of skis and within 20 minutes you're in this environment that people from anywhere on the planet with a love of nature would think is awesome.

'You can wander up the river 10 minutes from the village with a fishing rod in your hand, go to Dead Horse Gap and take off on the Cascade Trail out towards the Pilot Wilderness.

'You can take off in the car and have a picnic down at Geehi – take off in any direction,' Foster said.

The Kosciuszko National Park that surrounds Thredbo has astonishing natural qualities, from its alpine ranges above the tree line at around 1830m, to the sub-alpine snow gum forests and the ash forests and rivers in its lower reaches.

The KNP covers about 690,000 hectares and contains all the NSW alpine resorts. It runs from the Victorian border to the western edge of the Namadgi National Park in the Australian Capital Territory.

There's a fascinating tension between national parks and alpine resorts, between conservationists and developers. At the extremes, one side would have no alpine resorts, in fact, no trace of a human presence while the other side might release all the snowfields for development. But within those extremes, a common interest and common ground have been uncovered.

As much as they are charged with the conservation of the park, the land managers have always had an obligation to provide for recreation, for people to be able to use the natural assets.

The success of snow sports is testament to the demand there is for them and for that particular use of that terrain. David Osborn worked for the Kosciuszko National Park in the earlier part of his career, before he joined Kosciuszko Thredbo. He has a unique perspective.

'The community wants to be able to use Kosciuszko for the values that are associated with it, but it also wants to be able to use it for skiing.

'To me, it simply becomes an exercise of ensuring the environmental effects of the resort are contained within the resort.

'There were always green commandos who would have shut the Alpine Way at the park gate, but the original

DOWNHILL RIDES: *A mountain biker (left) hits the trail after riding the Kosciuszko Express, while Swedish skier Bengt Lke Danielsson (below) telemarks through spring snow off Mt Ramshead, with Mt Kosciuszko in the background.*

charter and successive plans of management always talked about the balance between conservation and development,' Osborn said.

Before the skiers, the Snowy Mountains' human visitors were generally motivated by economic and cultural objectives. The Aboriginal people of the Murray and Monaro areas and beyond were the earliest human visitors. Their visits were seen to coincide with the availability of bogong moths, upon which they would feast, but there is probably much more to it than that.

Tom Mitchell, who with his wife, the author Elyne Mitchell, was an enthusiastic explorer of the Snowy Mountains, was a grazier and a parliamentarian (from 1947 to 1976) on the Victorian side of the mountains, at Towong, near Corryong.

He saw the annual migration as having a much deeper purpose – social, religious and cultural.

'The popular reason given is to feast on the bogong moths but the real reason was far deeper than this. Firstly, there was no need to go to the high alps for food because at this time of the year, food was plentiful in the home bimbles (territories).

'Secondly, although well out of their bimbles, none of the Aborigines needed "passports" and thirdly, they carried no boomerangs or clubs or spears or any weapons.

'It is not generally known that this quiet, preoccupied dusky procession, entirely unarmed, going barefoot up the Khancoban Valley to the lonely heights of the high alps were performing a religious ceremony of deep and vital significance.

'The strange evocative quality of the pilgrimage up the Khancoban Valley is all the more interesting because the high alps were areas of menacing mystery to our Aborigines.

'They had a horror and dread of our alpine lands similar to the horror and dread the Maoris of New Zealand had for their mountains of Ruapehu and Tongariro in the North Island, which the Maoris firmly believed were peopled by huge terrible creatures half human and half revolting monsters.

'Accordingly, the annual visitation of our Aborigines to our high alps required not only a great deal of personal courage but a strong and unshakeable religious faith as well. Perhaps their faith in their god was stronger than our faith in ours,' (quoted in Young, page 74).

In the 1800s, the Aborigines were joined and eventually marginalised by gold miners and graziers. There are traces of diggings all along the Thredbo Valley.

Elyne Mitchell wrote that by the late 1800s, there was a 'road of sorts made along the Crackenback Range, on which bullock wagons could travel.'

She quoted from a report regarding an observatory established on Mt Koscisuzko by the Queensland Government meteorologist, Clement Wragge, and his party's journey to the peak.

They made their way past Merritts Camp, 'two thousand feet above Friday Flat in a distance of only about two miles.'

Wragge's offsider, Bernard de Burgh Newth 'became quite expert on Kiandra skis, with just the leather "stirrup" for a toe strap.'

Newth made 14 trips to Jindabyne for supplies during his 27 months at the Kosciuszko Observatory (from late 1897 to 1899) and Mitchell quotes him as expressing the need

to sometimes make the trip from Kosciuszko to Friday Flat in the dark '… it has been successfully negotiated at night, carrying one ordinary kerosene lantern, a moonless night at that,' (Mitchell, p102).

As Elyne Mitchell points out, this kind of venture becomes all the more respectable when contrasted with the quality and simplicity of the trails and equipment currently available.

She doesn't give Wragge and his party the status of being the first skiers on Thredbo's slopes however. That belongs to Charles Kerry and company. Kerry grew up on a sheep station between Bombala and Cooma. Along with Edgar Holden and 11 others, he made the ascent from Friday Flat on August 18, 1897 to Mt Kosciuszko, the first known winter ascent of Australia's summit, struggling up Merritts Spur through the snow and undergrowth.

They made the summit early in the afternoon and then turned tail for home. 'The return was easy,' Kerry wrote. 'We sat on our skis and tobogganed swiftly down slopes that had taken much labour in the morning,' (Mitchell, pp91-102).

Thredbo is a springboard; thousands have ventured beyond its slopes in winter, ridden the Kosciuszko Express chair and then scaled Australia's summit; millions have made the journey in summer.

In so many ways, the vision of Thredbo's pioneers has been fulfilled. They were drawn by the potential in its skiing, its long runs and rich vertical drop, the natural fit of the village in the valley and the scope beyond winter.

Their confidence in the enterprise was fuelled by their belief that others would share their vision and their passion for the mountains. They were right.

WHITE OPEN SPACES: *Skiers were scaling the Ramshead Range on their way to the summit of Australia in the late 1890s. Charles Kerry is credited with the first winter ascent of Mt Kosciuszko, on a route that went up the Merritts Spur in August 1897.*

Bibliography/sources/further reading

Books

Alan Andrews, *Skiing the Western Faces, Kosciusko*, Tabletop Press, 1993.

Barbara Cameron-Smith, *Wildguide Plants & Animals of the Australian Alps*, Envirobook, 1999.

Alec Costin, Max Gray, Colin Totterdell, Dane Wimbush, *Kosciuszko Alpine Flora*, CSIRO/Collins, 1979 (reprinted in 2000).

Jim Darby and Robert Upe, *The Snow Guide to Australia and New Zealand*, Explore Australia, 2005.

Stuart Diver with Simon Bouda, *Survival*, Macmillan, 1999.

Ian Foster and Ross Dunstan, *The Snowy Mountains*, Australian Geographic, 2002.

Geehi Club, *Snowy Mountains Walks*, Geehi Club, Cooma, 1962.

Noel Gough, *Mud, Sweat and Snow*, published by Noel Gough, 1994.

Tim Hall with photography by Trisha Dixon, Cornstalk Publishing, *Banjo Paterson's High Country*, 1992.

Klaus Hueneke, *Kosciusko Where the Ice-Trees Burn*, Tabletop Press, 1990.

Klaus Hueneke, *People of the Australian High Country*, Tabletop Press, 1994.

Peter Kabaila, *High Country Footprints*, Pirion Publishing, 2005.

John Landy, *Close to Nature*, Currey O'Neill Ross, 1985.

Craig McGregor, photographs by Helmut Gritscher, *The High Country*, Angus & Robertson, 1967.

Ian Mansergh and Linda Broom, *The Mountain Pygmy Possum*, UNSW Press, 1994.

Elyne Mitchell, *Discoverers of the Snowy Mountains*, Macmillan, 1985.

NSW National Parks and Wildlife Service, *Kosciusko Grazing, a History*, NPWS, 1991.

Tony Sponar, *Snow in Australia? That's News To Me*, Tabletop Press, 1995.

Helen Swinbourne, *Accordions in the Snow Gums: Thredbo's Early Years*, Thredbo Historical Society, 2006.

Rick Walkom, *Skiing Off the Roof*, Arlberg Press, 1991.

Judy Young, *Memories of Old Jindabyne*, Snowy River Shire Historical Society, 1993.

Michael Young, *The Aboriginal People of the Monaro*, NSW Department of Environment and Conservation, 2000.

Oswald Ziegler/The Council of the Shire of Snowy River, *Snowy Saga*, Oswald Ziegler Publications, 1960.

Magazines

Australian Ski Yearbook, various editions held in the Thredbo Historical Society and National Alpine Museum of Australia (Mt Buller) collections.

Jim Darby, "The World Cup goes downunder" *Airways* magazine, Qantas, July/August 1989 pp33-36.

Ski Extra/ExtraVert magazines, 1984-2000, various editions, author's private collection.

theSKImag, 2001-2006, various editions, author's private collection.

Newsletters

Thredbo Alpine Club, March 2004 and March 2005

Reports and plans

Derek Hand, *Report of the Inquest Into the Deaths Arising From the Thredbo Landslide*, Coroner's Court, NSW, 29 June 2000.

Clive Lucas, Stapleton & Partners, *Thredbo Alpine Village Conservation Plan*, Prepared for Kosciuszko Thredbo Pty Ltd, 1997.

NSW National Parks and Wildlife Service, *Report on the Proposed Thredbo Village Master Plan*, April 1989.

NSW National Parks and Wildlife Service, *Proposed Variations to the Determined 1988 Thredbo Village Master Plan, EIS, report by the determining authority*, July, 1994.

NSW National Parks and Wildlife Service, *2006 Plan of Management, Kosciuszko National Park*, June 2006.

Visual

Susie Diver, *Interview with Dick Dusseldorp*, 1995, VHS, Kosciuszko Thredbo collection, 1995.

Helen Malcher, *Charles Anton, the Main Range & Thredbo 1950-1962*, DVD, Home Studios, 2006.

Campaign Palace, *Thredbo Advertising Collection*, VHS.

Rebel Penfold-Russell, *Tommy Tomasi, A Life Well Travelled*, DVD, Rebelstudio, 2006.

Internet

Asia-Pacific Institute for Toponymy, www.apit.mq.edu.au

Australian Dictionary of Biography Online, www.adb.online.anu.edu.au

Disabled WinterSportAustralia, www.disabledwintersport.com.au

Geebung Ski Club, www.geebungskiclub.com.au

Hansard, Parliament of Australia, www.aph.gov.au/hansard

Happy Wanderers Ski Club, www.wanderersskiclub.com.au

Lend Lease, www.lendlease.com

Redbank Ski Lodge, www.redbankskilodge.com.au

Roslyn Lodge, www.roslynlodge.com.au

The Royal Australian Institute of Architects, www.architecture.com.au

Thredbo, www.thredbo.com.au

Thredbo Alpine Club, www.tac.org.au

Thredbo Ski Patrol, www.thredboskipatrol.org.au

Archives and collections

National Alpine Museum of Australia, Mt Buller, www.nama.org.au

Thredbo Historical Society, and in particular its John Gam collection (the Thredbo Museum is open 10am to 4pm daily between Boxing Day and Australia Day and on weekends and public holidays from February to April).

Interviews/oral histories

Unless otherwise specified in the text or below, all people quoted were interviewed by the author in 2006. Exceptions are:
Bill (William Samuel) Bursill – interviewed by Edith Swift, 2002, Thredbo Historical Society collection.
(Alexandra) Sasha Nekvapil – interviewed by Edith Swift, 2006, Thredbo Historical Society collection.
Harry Seidler, interviewed by Helen Dalley in "Deconstructing Harry", Nine Network *Sunday* program, October 11, 1998.
http://sunday.ninemsn.com.au/sunday/cover_stories/transcript_272.asp

Photography and image credits

Where there is more than one photograph or image on a page, if they are from separate sources, they are credited in a clockwise direction from bottom left.
Pages
Front cover: Geoffrey Hughes; Back cover: Reader Family collection; 1 Thredbo Historical Society (THS); 3 Mike Edmondson; 5 Kosciuszko Thredbo (KT)/Mike Edmondson; 6 KT/Mike Edmondson; 8 THS; 11 Geoffrey Hughes; 12 Australian Ski Yearbook; 13 Australian Ski Yearbook; 14 Ron Molnar; 16 Geoffrey Hughes; 17 Reader Family/Alan Hedges; 18 Kosciuszko Thredbo (KT)/Mike Edmondson; 21 Sydney Morning Herald/THS, Mark Ashkanasy/tSm; KT/Daryl Jackson Robin Dyke,; 26 Mark Ashkanasy/tSm; 27 Mark Ashkanasy/tSm; 28 Mark Ashkanasy/tSm; 29 Ross Dunstan; 30 KT; 32 Mark Ashkanasy/tSm; 33 KT; Max Dupain, Harry Seidler collection, State Library of NSW; 35 Mark Ashkanasy/tSm; 36 KT; 37 KT; 38 KT; 39 KT; 40 Ross Dunstan; 42 KT; 43 KT; 44 Geoffrey Hughes; 46 Geoffrey Hughes; 47 Geoffrey Hughes; 48 KT; 49 Geoffrey Hughes; 50 KT; 51 Roger Andrew, KT collection, KT; 52 KT; 53 Tommy Tomasi, Ross Dunstan; 54 KT; 55 Reader Family Collection/Douglass Baglin, THS, Mark Ashkanasy/tSm; 57 KT; 58 KT; 59 Geoffrey Hughes; 60 Roger Andrew; 61 Mark Ashkanasy/tSm; 62 Mark Ashkanasy/tSm; 63 Mark Ashkanasy/tSm; 64 Tomasi; 65 KT; 66 Tomasi; 67 Ross Dunstan; 68 Geoff Sawyer/Cary Pogson; 70 KT collection/Margot Seares; 73 Sun News Pictorial/National Alpine Museum of Australia; 74 THS; 75 THS; 76 Geoffrey Hughes; 77 Geoffrey Hughes; 78 THS; 79 Brian Chater/Redbank; 80 Tommy Tomasi; 81 Tommy Tomasi; 82 Tommy Tomasi; 83 KT; 84 Geoffrey Hughes; 85 THS; 86 KT collection/Margot Seares; 88 Geoffrey Hughes, Reader Family Collection/Douglass Baglin; 89 Mark Ashkanasy/tSm; 90 Mark Ashkanasy/Alpine Images; 91 Mark Ashkanasy/Alpine Images; 92 Tony Harrington/tSm; 94 KT; 95 KT/James Moore; 96 Ross Dunstan; 99 Mark Ashkanasy/tSm; 100 KT collection/Mike Edmondson; 103 KT; 104 KT; 105 THS; 106 KT; 107 KT/Brent Lynch; 108 KT; 109 THS; 110 KT; 111 KT; 112 KT; 113 Mike Edmondson; 114 Ross Dunstan; 115 KT collection/Ross Dunstan; 116 KT; 117 Mike Edmondson; 118 KT/Mike Edmondson; 126 KT/Mike Edmondson; author on dustjacket, Mark Ashkanasy/tSm.

Photographer websites

Mark Ashkanasy, www.aimage.com.au
Ross Dunstan, www.radexposures.com.au
Mike Edmondson, www.mikeedmondson.com.au
Brent Lynch, www.brentlynch.net
Ron Molnar, www.ronmolnar.com.au

tSm Publishing

Thredbo 50 was produced for Kosciuszko Thredbo by tSm Publishing, publishers of theSKImag.
Publishers: Jim Darby, Lou Pullar
Photo editor: Mark Ashkanasy, Alpine Images
Design and creative: Anthony Pearsall, Typographics
Sub editors: Mary Kerley, Robert Upe
tSm Publishing Pty Ltd, ABN 59 100 113 988
12 Alton Road (PO Box 146) Mt Macedon, Victoria, Australia, 3441
Go to: www.theskimag.com

Acknowledgements

Everybody spoken to for assistance in the creation and development of this work gave their cooperation instantly and willingly. In particular, the author is grateful to these people for their recollections and resources: Denise Allardice, Roger Andrew, Colin Battersby, Jono Brauer, Sam Brantsma, Marnie Brennan, Reg Bryson, Kim Clifford, Jane Coleman, Andrew Cocks, Philip Cullen, Rob de Castella, Euan Diver, Susie Diver, Cheryl Dunstan, Ross Dunstan, Robin Dyke, Mike Edmondson, Margaret Franke-Williams, Ron Finneran, Ian Foster, Andrew Harrigan, Nicole Hain, Flavia Hodges, Graeme Holloway, Adam Hosie, Geoffrey Hughes, Wayne Kirkpatrick, Ann Koeman, Cees Koeman, David Kuhn, Helen Malcher, David Milliken, Michael Milton, John Mitchell, Ron Molnar, Jayson Onley, David Osborn, Lorraine Packett, Rebel Penfold-Russell, Noni Plewes, Frank Prihoda, Nic Reader, Paul Reader, Heinz Reichinger, Michelle Reichinger, Maureen Roberts, Alan Rydge, Geoff Sawyer, Margot Seares, Werner Siegenthaler, Brad Spalding, Helen Swinbourne, Peter Tomasi, Tommy Tomasi, Robert Upe, Albert van der Lee, Christina Webb, Randy Wieman. Some of these people were also extremely generous in giving their time to help with the initial reading of the text.

The author also thanks these organisations and their people: Kosciuszko Thredbo Pty Ltd, National Alpine Museum of Australia, NSW National Parks & Wildlife Service, Thredbo Historical Society/Friends of Thredbo, State Library of NSW.
He also thanks the people he's skied with at Thredbo, especially Doug Chatten, Chris Gadsden, Julie Higman, Peter Ilinsky, Jay Kelly, Vanessa Knee and Peter Stone who have shared some of the mountain's secrets with him.
The author expresses his gratitude to his parents, Geoff and Heather Darby for getting him above the snow line in the first place and thanks his family for their continued encouragement for his indulgence in things to do with mountains (and expresses his delight whenever they share it) – Marnie Brennan and Olivia, Patrick, Cosmo and Joanna Darby.

A note on spelling

The Kosciusko Hotel has never been named the Kosciuszko Hotel and for most of its 50 years, Kosciuszko Thredbo did without the 'z' in its name. However, for consistency, we have used the spelling adopted in the 1990s to more accurately reflect the name of the Polish national hero, General Tadeusz Kosciuszko after whom the explorer Pawel Strzelecki named Australia's highest peak.

Index